By the Grace of God

A Memoir of WWII
from Yugoslavia to America

By the Grace of God

A Memoir of WWII
from Yugoslavia to America

Katharine Buschbacher De Kay

ISBN: 978-0-9978961-6-9

Library of Congress Control Number: 2018930580

Cover design by The Cheerful Word

Published by The Cheerful Word
224 Thompson St. #259
Hendersonville, NC 28792-2806

Order additional copies at www.Amazon.com

CR

Dedication

I dedicate this book to my parents in gratitude for their vision, courage and determination to bring their children to a better place for a bright future.

To my children and siblings, I say I am proud of the responsible citizens you have become, especially my brother for serving our country in war in Vietnam.

Contents

Chapter One
Memories of Indjija, The Kingdom of Yugoslavia,
My Birthplace (1932-1944) 1
Chapter Two
The Nazi Era (1942 to 1944) 17
Chapter Three
Fleeing Indjija to Ruma (October 1944) 23
Chapter Four
Landing in Upper Austria, near St. Polten (Fall/Winter 1944) 37
Chapter Five
Fleeing Again: Becoming Hobos (Early Spring 1945) 43
Chapter Six
The Grandeur of the Tirolean Mountain Top (1945) 47
Chapter Seven
The War is Over! (1945) 51
Chapter Eight
Kufstein, Austria: DP Camp (1945) 55
Chapter Nine
Transfer to Lager Haiming (1946 to 1947) 61
Chapter Ten
Free at Last! American Sector of Austria (Winter 1947) 67
Chapter Eleven
Hellbrunn: Countess von Rohn de Cais (1947-49) 87
Chapter Twelve
Salzburg and Captain Brody's Home (1949-1951) 99
Chapter Thirteen
Bremerhaven, Germany: Waiting for America (1951-1952) 107
Chapter Fourteen
Crossing the Ocean in 10 Days 113
Chapter Fifteen
Far Rockaway (Spring-summer 1952) 121
Chapter Sixteen
Moving to Manhattan (Summer 1952) 127
Chapter Seventeen
From Miss to Mrs. to Mother (1954) 143
Chapter Eighteen
Moving to Howard Beach (1958) 153
Reflections on Family 167

CR

Introduction

I am writing this book to inform first-generation Americans of the lives of their parents before WWII and why and how they got to America from countries all over the world, but could not go "home" again.

I am not alone in having lost my homeland when the Kingdom of Yugoslavia was destroyed in 1942-1944. Hungarians, Romanians, Poles, Czechs, and Slovakians were also conquered. All of these countries have Donauschwaben, or Volksdeutsche; German-speaking people, never having been German Nationals. We all belonged to the Austro/Hungarian Empire, which lost two thirds of its land to these aforementioned lands after WWI. Being a proud people, our culture carried on under another ruler, the same as before.

I have read several *Heimat* (Homeland) books in German, but found that many younger Generations cannot read German. My English language book will be enlightening to all who wonder who the Donauschwaben were. It is my hope and my wish that humankind will never experience a war like WWII again.

All of our cherished traditions ended in 1944 when we had to flee for our lives. Along with all our possessions, we also left behind the life we knew, the friends we had, the animals we loved, and still, we feel blessed that our family was together and made it through the war years healthy.

We were given a chance for a new beginning in America ten years later. We have learned and passed down new traditions so that our children could be like all the other children on the block, and we keep a few of our favorite homeland traditions alive to create memories for our family, treasuring the special bond we had with our parents. My children were lucky to grow up with four grandparents as all of them lived past the age of 90. They heard many a tale of what we did at home in our beloved Indjija, Yugoslavia.

The stories in these pages are meant to honor not just my life, but the thousands who no longer have a homeland, and yet, have created a home in this land of America. We are proud to be citizens here, even as we hold the home of our birth close in our hearts.

CR

Chapter One

Memories of Indjija, The Kingdom of Yugoslavia, My Birthplace (1932-1944)

My mother was so kind to people, she even gave the Gypsies a
chicken every time they came through our town,
even though she told me to lock the front gate,
which was always open at other times.

Franz Bachert was born on January 29, 1905, and Maria Brucker was born on August 23, 1908—they were my parents. They were married in 1927 in Indjija, Yugoslavia in the Catholic Church of St. Peter and St. Paul. Then, they signed on as domestic servants for a year or so, in France. They saved money to build the first part of their house, a single room and kitchen in Indjija on Lastina Uliza *broy deved* (Serbian for Lastina Street number 9). My Dad taught me to say that at a very young age, so I could

Maria Brucker (19) Franz Bachert (22)
Wedding Day Indjija, 1927

tell people where I lived in case I got lost. Our town was a mix of nationalities: Germans, Serbians, Croatians, Hungarians, and Jews, all living harmoniously from 1825 to1944, even before it became Yugoslavia. This land was part of the Austro/Hungarian Empire until after WWI. When Mom and Dad needed more money, they worked again as domestic servants in Serbia for a minister in the government. This is where their second child, Franz, was born, but he lived only a month. My older sister, Maria, was 18 months old when she died from whooping cough. So, when I came along as the third and only child for six years, till my sister Anna was born, I was the princess in the family. I was born Katharina Bachert on July 11, 1932. (All of the important family names and dates are entered into the family bible for reference.)

Dad's mother, Juliana Flehr Bachert, was a widow; his father, Adam Bachert died from gunshot wounds he received fighting for the Austrian empire during WWI. The land where they lived, Indjija, was then in the Kingdom of Yugoslavia, not Austria. So, she did not have the right to financial assistance for her three young children Franz, Adam, and Katharina. Dad was the oldest, and at 14 years old when his father died, he became the breadwinner for the family. Oma Bachert was French. She washed laundry for people; that is my memory of her at home in Indjija. Later, when Dad had a family of his own, his brother took over the role as breadwinner. I remember whenever my Adam *Batchi* (Hungarian for uncle) paid his mother's monthly grocery bill in the *Armbruster* (local store), which was around the corner from my house, he got a sack of hard candy for me. We called it *Side Zucker,* because it was smooth as silk (*side* means silk).

During vacation from school, I was sent to my mother's step-family. Johann Brucker was my mom's father, whose wife died when Mom was only two. There, I was once again a princess, as my mom's stepbrother and stepsister, Onkel Franz and Tante Lissi, never married. I guess they saw enough trouble between their parents to stay away from marriage. I remember Mom telling me that she and Dad sent money home to her father to save up for their house, but when they came home from Serbia, it was all gone. Her father apparently drank his *Most* (hard cider) with it. Somehow, they still managed to build a very nice house for us, surrounded by a large vegetable garden, and fruit trees. They also kept chickens, geese, and ducks. Emma, the goat was as old as I was, and she gave milk for the family for many years. My parents bought four piglets every spring, in hopes of raising them to sell at least one, sometimes two, and earn a nice nest egg in return. Two or three pigs were butchered and smoked for the family's use all year.

My grandfather, Opa Brucker, put a tin barrel in the yard, and all the fruit that fell from the trees was put in this barrel till winter. He then took it to the *Spiritus Fabrick* in Indjija; a distillery that made whiskey.

My Opa Brucker lived with us most of my life, as he and his new wife never got along. He considered my mom his only true kin. Mom and Dad put schnapps into tea when it was cold and snowy in winter. Grandfather drank it like it was it was a brandy called *Slivovic,* which was made from pure spirits with nothing added, but fruit. As an adult, we sold it in the liquor store my husband Larry and I owned in Jamaica, Queens, New York. It was called

Larry's Liquors. Jews, mostly, bought schnapps, as it was a custom to wish each other well over a glass of the stuff during the holidays. Only people from that region of the world know about Slivovic. It is pure and kosher. In America, bourbon is a similar drink.

We had a large crop of pears from our trees, which we sold in the summer. Neighbors sold or bartered extra items they had for things they needed. I remember Dad, as a stone mason, made a marble table for a friend, the barber, who came every Saturday to our house to shave and trim Dad's mustache. It was payment for that table. I had a swing on the pear tree, and I loved to sing while I was swinging. My neighbors said to me in German, *"Katl, du kannst so schön singe."* ("Katl, you can sing so beautifully."). So, I sang even louder the next time. They also said to me on my way to church, *"Na Hat Die Mutter nix andres zu tun wie mit deine haar zu spiele?"* ("Does your mother have nothing better to do than play with your hair?") She always put rags into my hair after washing it on a Saturday night. By Sunday morning, they made lovely curls for church that lasted all day, and I wore ribbons in my hair, that were made from the same material as my dress.

There are so many wonderful memories of home in Indjija. I was taught to make little samplers. A sampler is material embroidered with backstitch in colorful thread, usually with cute sayings on them. Red was my favorite color. Samplers were hung on the wall either in the back, or side, of the stove to keep the splatters off the wall, and also in the kitchen where you washed your hands. They were hung up especially when guests came, to keep the wall looking clean and nice. Also, you can get a smile from the clever verse.

Another memory is from early spring when Mom brought baby chicks into the kitchen after they hatched in the barn to keep them warm and make them grow up fast for our Sunday dinners. It was fun to play with them, and we had to be careful not to step on them, as we walked around our combined kitchen and Anna's and my bedroom. This kitchen was only used in winter, as we had a whole kitchen, laundry room and bathroom complex at the end of the house to use during warm weather. There was also a large iron stove, not a small enamel one like in this winter kitchen. The bathroom had a bathtub which we filled and emptied with a pail, because there was no running water in the house. The toilet was still an outhouse far to the back of the property. The laundry room had a large kettle built into a brick oven, where the water was heated to use in the bathtub, and the laundry tubs. It was the place to hang-out, except during extremely cold weather.

Winter time was spent in this warm kitchen in the front of the house. As soon as we could hold the needles, Mom would show us how to darn socks, and knit mittens, socks, and scarfs, or sweaters. We helped Mom make braided rugs by cutting up used clothing. We cut strips, which then Mom sewed together into oval rugs for our feet on the cold floor, as we got out of bed. Very little was discarded in our home. We had a Singer sewing machine with foot pedals. Mom made nearly all of our clothes. The only store-bought dresses we had were the ones we got on credit from the local department store owner in Indjija, who gave out his stock items when we were waiting to be evacuated. In 1944, Anna and I each picked out a knitted dress that we packed to take with us. We gave him an IOU to pay for them, when we got back home. The storeowner's name was Zech; his name is still engraved into the marble slab over his building. He knew his merchandise would be plundered, as soon as the townspeople left. So, it was better to give it away with the promise of someday being paid, than to lose it to the enemy; the Tito Partisans in the wheat fields outside of town.

We had an underground cement cistern at the edge of the house to collect rainwater from the roof for our household use. My mother said the rainwater made hair very soft and shiny, and was much better for your hair than well water. We had a separate well for drinking and cooking water. It was next to the walnut tree, and across from the winter garden in front of the brick wall, that surrounded our property. The well had a wooden lattice cover. It looked like a house with a wheel on the side, and a pail inside the lattice-shaped house. It was a good life, and we were mostly self-sufficient by raising geese, ducks, and chickens, and growing fruit and vegetables. The pigs we raised, we slaughtered for smoked meats and sausage to last all winter. The flour for noodles, bread, and strudels, my parents earned during harvest time for helping the neighboring farmers bring in their wheat. By now, we had two bedrooms added on to the original house, along with the *wintergarten*, which was a glass-enclosed veranda. It ran, the whole length of the house, to store the plants in winter. We called it a *glasgang*, because the walls were made of glass.

My father was a stone mason by trade. He made floor tiles in his place of work, the *Steinmetz Fabrick von Willi Schwartz*. We had

Franz Bachert, Stone masons
Indjija, 1937

tiles all through the wintergarten. It was very pretty with all the flowers over-wintering in there. My parents let a Muslim man from Bosnia sleep there every fall. His name was Franjo. He came to help the neighboring farmers, alongside my parents, harvest the abundant wheat crop. He had eight children, who had nothing to eat, he said. My mother encouraged him to raise animals to help feed his family. But he said it was a rugged, stony environment where he lived, and he could not even grow grass. He said, if his children saw a blade of grass come through the rocks, they would eat it. Where we lived in Yugoslavia was fertile ground. We never knew that some parts of this beautiful land harbored such hunger. We had everything we wanted to eat in Indjija.

My mother was so kind to people, she even gave the Gypsies a chicken every time they came through our town, even though she told me to stay inside and lock the front gate, which was always open at other times.

When I was still a child of nine or ten, I went with my parents into the wheat fields at harvest time. It was my job to lay down the ties before they came with an arm full of wheat to tie into bundles. They went earlier than I did, so a neighbor, Liss *Bessl* (Mrs. Liss) was to take me in when I woke up. She came across the street for me several times, but I did not get up all day. She told other neighbors I must be sick, as I did not eat, or get out of bed all day. She did not know what to do. She brought me soup, but I did not eat it, and she was worried. By the time my parents came home from the field that night, Liss Bessl was so upset and embarrassed at what happened. My mother asked me what was wrong with me, and I said, "Nothing, I did not want to go with Liss Bessl, because her mouth looks crooked." The next day, they made another neighbor responsible for looking after me. But, as soon as they could, they took me with them into the field for the day.

Mom and Dad left early each day for a week or more, until all the wheat was harvested. It got very hot during the day, so they wanted to work while it was cooler in the morning. It took about an hour to ride out to the wheat field, and by the time they arrived, it was just about sunrise. Franjo received wheat for payment, just like my parents did. Another man also came from Bosnia during the summer to sell ice cream. He was Muslim, and wore a white suit with a red fez. We called him *sladolet* man (ice cream man). He went through every street calling out "Sladolet!" So, we all ran to get money from our parents to buy sladolet. It was the only time we had something so cold, as we had no freezers or even refrigerators. Only the basement was cool enough for storing milk and cheese for a short while. We also stored vegetables from our garden there over the winter.

In later years in New York, my husband Lorenz (Larry) Buschbacher, who was also from Indjija, told his mother that he used to trade eggs from his mother's hens for sladolet. She always wondered why her hens suddenly did not lay eggs anymore. When she found out, she had a good laugh.

My parents went often to the *Grosse Wirtshaus* (large restaurant) by the name of *Kölln, for large festive parties.* Smaller parties were held outside in the picnic grounds, when the weather was warm, so children could go too. Men sometimes put a twig of rosemary in the lapel of their suit, especially when going to a party where drinking and dancing was taking place. It was mostly for not smelling the smoke, as men rolled their own tobacco into cigarettes when they smoked at parties. The music was always a brass band with harmonica. Many weddings and funeral meals were held at home. A large bedroom was emptied of the furniture, and then filled with tables and chairs from neighbors to make it into a dining room. Neighbors also did the cooking, and brought the food in time for dinner when the bridal couple came home from church. There was a procession with music through the town. After dinner, dancing took place in another room, or outside if the weather was warm. A common present to the bride and groom was a poem written by the parents, and recited by their child. It always was an inspirational message with good wishes for the future. I was often asked to recite such a poem, which I loved to do.

Often, during summer, men went through the town selling fish from the Danube River. The towns of Stara Pasowa or Becska were about two hours away, and it was not often that we got to go there. Larry, as a young boy, and his mother, Rosina Busch-bacher, spent weeks in those towns during the summer, as they were wellness resorts for people with arthritis. The Danube was thought to have healing waters. Lenzi, as they called him then, learned to swim there. So, the rest of the summer he could swim in Grundloch, a natural spring in the outskirts of Indjija. Girls never went there, as far as I know, but the boys loved it.

At our house, in the wintergarten there was also *die Speis* (a pantry). It was the room which held all of our canned fruits and vegetables on its shelves. It was a colorful sight. Every fall, my mom canned some of our vegetables and fruits to eat during the winter months. The sauerkraut we kept down in the basement, because of its pungent aroma. In the basement, there were also potatoes and horseradish roots, cabbages, apples, nuts, and all other food items needed to have a good life year-round.

I remember the year 1942, when the Germans came to town during the occupation of Yugoslavia. It became fashionable to drink beer. We grew grapes in our region of the world, and Hungarian wine is still coveted by wine connoisseurs. We never drank beer. Somehow, it made us better Germans to eat dishes with dark bread and more potatoes, with not so much meat or *Knödl* (boiled dumplings), and *Strudel* (layered pastry). That was Austro/Hungarian cuisine, not German. So, my mother made beer and put it into bottles to let it ferment in the basement. One time, she sent me down to the basement for something, when I saw a disaster. Every beer bottle had popped open and white foam was gushing out all over everything. The cleanup was a chore for all of us. That was the end of beer making, and my parents went back to drinking wine with Sunday dinners. Even children got a little wine mixed with club soda, as we had no soft drinks. It was much later, in about 1940/41, when a factory opened up which bottled fruit extract to make syrup for flavoring club soda.

I often was sent to the wine merchant with a pitcher to buy wine for dinner. I was taught to say this in Serbian. *Zirna* means red and *blanco* means white. We had a harmonious life with our Serbian and Jewish neighbors until 1942. We each had separate places of school and worship, but were respectful and socialized with each other, even when some of our German neighbors thought we should not do this anymore. They thought we should be more respectful of the Third Reich.

In that year, the men from the neighborhood, who didn't own a radio, came together in front of our house at 7:00 pm to listen to the news with my father. It seemed a war was raging all over Europe, but Yugoslavia was neutral. I was almost 10 years old and suspected something was not right, even though I was never told about the war in Europe either at home or at school. Shortly afterwards, we heard that the synagogue went up in flames and the Serbian king's statue was torn down in the park. These places were on the path my father had to take on his way to the *Steinmetz Fabrick*, the factory where he worked. He walked there and back until later, when he had a bike. He rode his bike there in the morning and came home for lunch at noon. He took a nap on the floor of the master bedroom, because my Mom did not let him mess up the bed. At 2:00 pm he pedaled back to work till 7:00 pm. We were worried about his safety, and mine. I had to come straight home from school, and was not able to play with anybody. My mother was fearful of the parents of my friends. She did not know whom to trust with your thoughts in those days; it was neighbor against neighbor. She separated us from everyone.

Soon tanks, trucks, and motorcycles, rows and rows of them arrived riding noisily through the main street of town. One person raised a hand in protest and was shot dead right there, no questions asked. Everyone stepped back quietly, and went home. The parade was over. Soon the young men were called to the town hall, where they were loaded on a train, and sent to Germany as *volunteers*. My father's brother was one of them. I never saw him again. They were not volunteers; they were kidnapped. My father's boss was one of them also. After, his departure, my father was promoted to head of the factory. It was an important job. As he was already over 40 years old, he was excused from serving the Vaterland. Later in the war, as they ran out of young men, they took everyone into service. It was called *Volksturm* (people's storm). Larry's parents had connections and money. They were able to get their oldest son, Valentin, who was 18 years old, a job in Greece building an airport for the German Army. It saved him from being drafted—kidnapped. Larry was just twelve years old, and so he was also spared. We were never German Nationals; how could this have happened?

Life, as we knew it, was over in October of 1942. Our king was exiled to England, and we, who did not leave our homes, were now subjects of Nazi Germany. Life had changed; somehow, I knew it was not good. Jews closed their shops and left town. But

I had no idea what was to happen next. But first, I have more happy memories to share from my youth.

Christmas in Indjija

In the olden days, we made our Advent Calendars at home or school. We had religious education, only Catholic, every day in grammar school. During the Nazi Occupation, I do not remember having religion taught in school. In fact, going to church was discouraged. Also, the plays put on by the nuns every year were forbidden. These were major productions enjoyed by all the residents of Indjija. I often performed in these plays and enjoyed it. We also had a live Nativity every year, which was also forbidden by the Nazis. The nuns disappeared. The kindergarten they ran closed up. The young priest left, only Hans Pfarrer was left as he was a native son and the main priest of our church. I remember Mom lit candles and prayed a lot during those times.

Top row, (L end) Käthe Bachert, Play depicting wheat harvest, Spielschule, Indjija, 1938

At Christmas, we decorated a real tree with heirloom ornaments and cubed sugar wrapped in silver tissue paper with fringe on both ends and a red ribbon. When he was a boy, my clever husband, Lenzi, took out the sugar cubes, ate them, and replaced them with buttons. His mother never knew about that either. I was not so smart, and my sister was too young to think of such things. We hung the same glass ornaments every year. We also used real candles in clip holders on the tree branches. But they were only lit when we all were together in the evenings around the Christmas tree. It was a festive time to sit around the tree and count our blessings, while singing carols, and telling Bible stories.

In my childhood home, as in all German-speaking countries, Christmas is a national holiday for two days, December 25th and 26th. Children and family are central to this holiday, and there are many wonderful traditions that go along with it. This is when families and friends get together to celebrate, to share the cookies and cakes mothers have spent baking for most of December, and to enjoy some *glühwein* (mulled wine) while singing Christmas carols.

We also had a walnut tree in our front yard, which gave us so many walnuts, that my mother sold some to the neighbors for baking at Christmas time. We ate nuts as snacks all winter long. During Christmas, we also roasted chestnuts which came from Greece, I think. I know the figs and oranges we ate came from Greece. We had very few of them since they were expensive. Our town had chestnut trees lining the *Allee* along the park. Before 1941, Indjija was a quiet place for strolling and meditating. After the invasion, no one put Christmas decorations on houses, only pine wreathes were hung on the doors by some.

Presents were given on Christmas Eve. There were no presents left under the tree leading up to Christmas Day. The Christ Child was not yet born, and since he was placed into the crib late at night, so were our gifts. Late in the evening, after dinner on Christmas Eve, the Christ Child arrived in person. We called Him *"Christkindl."* Sometimes neighbors got together to let the children play in one house, while the others decorated the tree. Every year in the midst of the celebrating, there was a knock on the door. In walked a white-robed, angel-like lady who represented the Christ Child. Her robes were a rolled-up apron, filled with candy, nuts, and apples. I always knew it was my mother, because I recognized her voice. All the children had to kneel in front of her and recite a prayer. She had a switch and tapped you on the head to remind you not to do bad things in school or at home. This Christkindl knew when you were naughty or did not pay attention in school and reminded us to do better next year. When she turned to leave, her apron unrolled and dropped its yummy contents. All of us kids excitedly gathered up the gifts she brought us. Each year, my dolly appeared again in new clothes, with freshly washed and curled hair. The parents came to fetch their children and see what the Christkindl left you at your house. Then, the whole family went to Midnight Mass.

The children showed off their new toys—my sister Anna and I got complementary presents, so we could play together and share. One year, Anna received a doll carriage, and I got the doll. We named her Crystl. We also received enamel pots and pans, but not many other toys that I can remember. Clothes were given more often, especially knitted items, because winter was cold and snow lasted most of the season. Mothers knitted sweaters, socks, shawls, hats, and mittens for the whole family. Mom also sewed our dresses and corduroy jumpers. Mostly, only useful toys were gifted, and were geared toward teaching physical work; tools for boys, cooking items for girls. Not many books were given either, only those needed as school supplies. Oral storytelling was common. Whenever my maternal grandfather and step-grandmother would fight, Opa

Käthe (12) & Anna (6) Bachert,
Lastina Ulica, Indjija
Christmas presents, 1943

Brucker would stay with us for the winter. He would tell us stories of his childhood without electricity, radios, or bicycles, and
how he had to walk long stretches in cold and snowy weather everywhere. Storytelling was the only joy he had, and he made up
so many tales. We should be thankful for the wonderful life we
have with all these modern conveniences. My Uncle Adam always told stories of his soccer matches. He was on a team called
Radnitca (I think that means workers in Serbian.).

Christmas Eve dinner was always *Mohnnudelns* (poppy seed
noodles) or *Nuss Nudeln* (broad, egg noodles sautéed in a sweet
poppy seed paste, or finely ground walnuts). It was a holy day,
when no meat was eaten according to the Catholic religion. On
Christmas Day, a roasted goose was traditionally served with
all the trimmings. Liver and sausage stuffing, red beet salad,
creamed spinach, and maybe some carrots saved from Mom's
garden in the fall. Then, more friends came to sample the baked
goods and gluhwein. The Christmas goose was given a handful
of corn many times during the day by me while we were fat-
tening her up for this wonderful meal. My mother picked out
the goose she wanted for Christmas dinner from our flock. She
separated the goose from the others, and put it into the front yard
by herself. Every time we passed the goose, she got some ground
corn. She ate all day long every day. By Christmas, she was very
fat and delicious.

The festivities continued and the tree stayed up till January 6th,
which is the Feast of the Three Kings, or the Feast of the Epiphany. We did not eat meat on any religious holidays. In fact, we
ate meat only on Sundays for most part of our lives. Only when
chickens got old enough to eat in the spring did we have meat
on Wednesdays, as well. Sometimes, Mom sent me to the butcher for a quarter pound of beef and marrow bones. This became

soup with farina knödl we called *"Löffel Knödl,"* because they were made by dipping a spoonful of dough into the boiling soup. These knödls were special because we only made them when we had beef for soup.

On the Feast of The Three Kings, we made doughnuts from yeast dough that had to rise for hours. This dough was rolled out, then shaped with a glass as doughnuts we called *Krapfen.* Coins were inserted into some of the doughnuts before frying them in hot fat then dusted them with powdered sugar and cinnamon. These doughnuts with coins in them represented the Three Kings that came with gifts to visit the Christ child in Bethlehem. As we ate the doughnugts, we were looking for the coins in hopes to find the biggest denomination of coin to have the distinction of being the most important king of the day. Quarters represented the high king, dimes for the middle king, and nickels for the lowliest king. Those who did not find any coins at all were not kings, and had to do their chores as usual.

The night before Epiphany, my father wrote on the front door of the house with chalk to welcome each of the Three Kings: K for Kaspar, M for Melchior, and B for Balthazar. It was thought at the time, that a king came from each continent, since there were only three known continents when Christ was born. We celebrated the Three Kings, who followed the special, comet-tailed star in the sky directing them to Bethlehem, where baby Jesus was born on January 6th and that marked the end of the Christmas season.

These are some of the memories of Indjija that I cherish. My childhood was so filled with wonder and joy, and I am glad the shock and hardship of the coming years never erased these happy times from my heart and my mind.

CR

Chapter Two

The Nazi Era (1942 to 1944)

*The Serbian and German people lived peacefully for five genera-
tions in Indjija, Yugoslavia, and I had known only peace.*

It was 1941. Some men in brown shirts and boots walked around our
town telling the Indjija inhabitants to get ready to welcome the men
of the Third Reich. The war was already raging all over Europe before
the Nazis invasion of Yugoslavia. The Serbian Army was no match for
the Nazi war machine, and they were quickly defeated. My father put
our radio on the window ledge to let the neighbors hear the news, and
they had lengthy discussions about what they heard. Rumor had it that
we would be next.

After the German soldiers invaded Indjija and people got used to seeing them everywhere—I think they were stationed in the Hungarian
School building that was not used anymore—they were friendly and
surprised to find German-speaking people in Yugoslavia. People invited them to dinner, and many officers were housed in the rich farm-

ers' large homes. This was a good thing for my father, as his boss
was made an adviser of sorts and went to Germany. My father was
promoted to director of the factory that made ceramic tiles and head-
stones. He traveled to Belgrade and other places to oversee the work
of installing tile floors for affluent people. He saw modern bathrooms
complete with bathtubs. We did not have bathtubs yet in Indjija. On
one trip, he brought a bathtub home for us. We had no indoor plumbing, yet we used it by heating water in the laundry tubs and carrying
buckets from the back of the house all the way to the laundry room
adjacent to the bathroom. The plumbing for the bathroom was not
installed before we were evacuated. The bathroom was made from
what was once was the chicken stall. It was whitewashed and made
good looking for such a gem as a large bathtub. All the stalls were an
extension of the living quarters, and were made of brick like the rest
of the house. My parents never borrowed money, but saved until they
had enough to do a job.

My mother worked in the tile factory sometimes, when there was a
rush order. She came home with different colored dust on her clothing, as she had to mixed the powders to make patterns on the tiles. She
loved doing this more creative work, and it also gave the family extra
money for special jobs on the house.

After Austria lost WWI, we became Yugoslavian Nationals. Our roots
go back about ten generations to Germany. It seems that after the fall
of the Ottoman Empire, the Austrian emperors encouraged settlement
of the Banat and Batschka (Hungary) to repopulate the area. The emperors offered the citizens free land and other benefits. Under Maria
Theresia, the Archduchess of Austria-Este, settlers received financial
support and long-term tax relief. The only requirement was to be Roman Catholic. The Turks trampled the earth during their attack on
Vienna, but Christian people who respected what God created, desired
to bring the land back to its fertile state, and it was the requirement

of the Hungarian landowners to be Roman Catholic like they were. The new farmers were told to plant vineyards and tend them well, as a given amount of crop had to be produced. If they failed, their land would be taken away. As it turned out, many had no time to tend their own land, as the master's land required all their time.

When Hitler occupied Yugoslavia, he had a program, *Heim ins Reich* (home to the Reich). All who wanted to leave foreign countries could move to Germany. My grandfather, Johann Brucker, and his son, Franz Brucker, went and worked in a factory for years. Luckily, my grandfather came home in time to help us evacuate in 1944. My Onkel Franz went home to Semlin to help his mother and sister evacuate. Opa always lived with us because he and his wife (my mother's stepmother) were separated. By then, our street names were changed to German names, and our town was now India, not the Serbian Indjija. My street became Gregor Brenner Gasse. In Serbian it was, and is now again, Lastina Uliza. Farmers were told how much wheat to give to the Fatherland. There was a collection place where they had to deliver it after harvest. The *Stiefel Manner* (boots men) kept track of all this. They suddenly became important people in town. I was now ten years old, and Anna was four.

The Serbian and German people lived peacefully for five generations in Indjija. The Jews were long gone by then. I had known only peace. In the 1800s, some of our ancestors came from the Black Forest region of Germany, and moved south to Austria-Hungary. That is where my Bachert name stems from; the Banat area of Hungary. Based on an 1833 census of the area, Bachert Stefan and wife Katharina Stadler arrived in Indjija from Prestovatz Banat in 1833. That is the first Bachert, a farmer in Indjija, on record. It also shows that twelve Jews lived there then. But now, even as a child of ten years old, I could tell people were increasingly nervous about something. The men gathered on the street around the front window of my house listening to Dad's radio, aggravated at what they heard each day. Their fists flying in the air, I was scared and stayed inside in wondering, "What is going on with my neighbors?" Little did I know, and never was I told, about the war spreading all over Europe and across to Africa.

The Desert Fox, General Erwin Rommel, ordered his tanks toward Egypt. In December 1942, Pearl Harbor, Hawaii, had been bombed by the Japanese, so now the Americans joined the war, and it became World War II. We in Yugoslavia were sheltered up until then. But soon, life as we knew it would be shattered. Some of our neighbors started wearing brown shirts and boots, telling neighbors we had to align with Germany and that Yugoslavia was no more, as Austria was now part of Germany also, and we should be welcoming the German soldiers as they will protect us from harm.

Meetings between the Stiefel Manner, as my mother called them, and the townspeople were held at auditoriums and the *sportplatz* (the sports field) in the evenings to explain what was happening in the world, and to encourage them to embrace the Third Reich. After all, we were Germans and needed to own up to that fact. My parents avoided these meetings, though my mother eventually attended one, and came home saying what a waste of time it was. Later, I heard her telling the other women on the block, that it was all about a rich land-owner's wife, who complained that her maid was wearing the same sweater as her daughter, saying, "The maid is a step below my daughter and the nerve that she can wear the same sweater; what a shame. Equality has gone a step too far for Indjija." That was the only time my mother went to a meeting, but we all found it disconcerting. Then, we had visits from a neighbor, who now considered himself an organizer for *Das Deutsches Reich*, the German Regime. He now wore the brown shirt and boots. To my mother and the other women in town, he gave some red silky material, and a smaller piece of black material to make the Nazi flag to hang out the window when the Germans came.

She took that material and made very beautiful gathered skirts for Anna and me. I remember this skirt and loved wearing it when we got to Austria. It was a silky kind of material, wrinkle free, easy to wash, and no ironing needed. It had three, one inch strips of black around the bottom and a broad, gathered waist band. It looked stunning with the white blouse that I wore to school in Austria.

So, now we children figured we knew what the excitement was all about—visitors! When a visitor is expected, my mother always made strudels and cookies. But she did not do this now, and we found it strange. Our normal life was giving way to something that just felt wrong. Everybody was on edge all the time. I was not allowed to go anywhere after school anymore, and the only friend I could see was my neighbor, Maria Turk.

The only place I could go to were my violin lessons. I met some of my friends there, as Herr Mayer was not only the music teacher in town, but he was also my fourth-grade teacher. He taught other instruments as well. I loved to hear my friends play the *Zieharmonika* (an accordion), as it was my favorite instrument. I asked to play it too, but my parents got a good deal on a used violin from a neighbor's son who outgrew it, so they bought me that instead. I loved any kind of music, and was thrilled to get it. It was my last year there, as next I went to *Bürgerschule* (secondary school). I loved Herr Mayer's class and was eager to learn music from him too. But science

Katharina Bachert, 3rd row, 4th to right of Herr Mayer, Volkschule, Indjija, 4th grade, 1942

was my all-time favorite. Creative writing and poetry became my favorite later in life. I was not exposed to books at home; we only had a
bible. The Countess von Rohn de Cais became my heroine for inspira-
tion later on.

I watched Herr Mayer's maid clean fish one afternoon, while waiting
for my lesson. I never saw fish in the Danube. The river was at least
two hours away from Indjija, and we never went there. My mother could not afford to buy from the fish vendors who brought fish
to town. They pushed their carts through the main streets shouting,
"Riba, Riba!" (fish in Serbian). The maid cleaned the fish by the well
in the yard, and we kids ran over to see it. It was a good way to get
to see a fish up close. I never would have seen one otherwise. It was
a carp. We inspected the scales, and she showed us his lungs (gills),
the openings on his sides. It was a hands-on science lesson, which we
should have been given credit for by Herr Mayer. It was a carefree
time in Indjija for us kids, but a stressful time for our parents. We did
not know what was waiting just around the corner.

CR

Chapter Three

Fleeing Indjija to Ruma (October 1944)

The men on patrol stayed active and alert at the edges of town
until all the women and children were safely delivered.
My father was also on patrol, so we packed the wagon
and set out for Ruma without him.

Soon, the quiet town of Indjija was awakened to the fact that war
was near, and coming closer every day.

In the capital city, Belgrade, there was a coup that overthrew the
government. The Yugoslavian ruler while the Prince Peter was
under age, his cousin Prince Paul, made a pact with Hitler. He
signed a treaty of alliance in Vienna. Prince Paul was overthrown
and the young Prince Peter, son of King Alexander, became the
rightful King of Yugoslavia. He opposed the deal. In retaliation,
the Nazis crucified a whole town in central Serbia killing eight
thousand high school students at once.

King Peter wanted to keep Yugoslavia out of the war, and he declared neutrality. After two years of neutrality it was shattered on April 6, 1941. The Nazis did not take, "No," for an answer. They attacked in central Serbia, King Peter's Royal Army was quickly defeated by Nazi forces. Now even King Peter's life was threatened and he had to flee to England for safety. In Indjija, the statues in the park of the Kings were beheaded and the synagogue set on fire. Notice was given to the people, "We are coming, like it or not." The Nazis defeated the Royal Army in a week in Central Serbia. They now marched into Belgrade and south to Indjija. This was Easter, April 10, 1942.

I saw my first airplane fly over our town. I admired it as I saw it dip a little, and again I watched in amazement when three large, black eggs came out of it over our new train station (we had two train stations). I watched in awe as a huge fire broke out where the eggs fell, and it was goodbye to our train station. Luckily, it was empty at the time and no one was killed. It was a Russian plane, given to the future ruler of the former Yugoslavia, Marshall Tito.

The train master was new in town, but did not live there. He rented our spare bedroom for his family's furniture in anticipation of an attack on the train station. Their daughter was a classmate of mine, and my first Protestant friend. Her name was Emily. Most of the Christian population in Indjija was Roman Catholic, except for the Serbians who were Russian Orthodox. Up till now, we all lived in harmony, with respect for each other. This came to an end when most of the Jews left after their synagogue went up in smoke that night. Some Serbians followed Tito into the wheat fields outside of town. The harmony among the Indjija population had irrevocably changed. Life as we once knew it, sadly no longer existed.

In school, we did a lot of calisthenics to build our strength. We were encouraged to practice this sport at home, as we needed to become strong in body and spirit to prepare us for whatever lay ahead, and what the Fuhrer wanted from us. Instead of visiting museums or other educational activities, our school trips now consisted of going into the fields collecting herbs for the wounded German soldiers. Mandatory sports festivals took place instead of church on Sunday mornings. My mother wrote notes to keep me home saying she was sick and needed me to stay and help her with my little sister. I resented not being able to spend time at the sportplatz with my friends. One did not know whom to trust, or what people were thinking, and she would not leave me with this unknown influence. I only attended school and music lessons, nothing else. Our Sundays were for family church days only, not for sports or herb collecting in the forest.

Elizabeth & Lissi Brucker,
Feeding piglets,
Semlin, Yugoslavia, 1939

I remember as a young child, before this all happened, I took the train to visit my mother's step-family in Semlin, a suburb of Belgrade. I saw Oma Brucker, her daughter, Tante Lissi, and her son, Onkel Franz. We went to Belgrade to some theatre performances my Tante Resca was in. Resca is a Serbian nickname for Theresia, which is German. She was one of my Opa Brucker's sisters, a well-liked actress in Belgrade. Opa also had a sister, Rosl, there She and her family also welcomed me always. They all liked to meet their kin from Indjija, especially their brother's child, Maria's family. Too bad Anna never had a chance to do this. At that time, she was too young. During the occupation, we could not go anywhere.

I also went by myself to Vukovar by train to visit my mother's only relative from her mother's side, Anton Gartner. Her mother, Katharina Gartner Brucker, died during childbirth when my mom was two years old. During the German Occupation, Anton got a job in government *Die Grossgespanschaft Vukovar*. He was well educated and spoke Serbian and German perfectly. He and his Croatian wife traveled through Indjija around Easter in 1941, shortly before the railroad station was bombed. My mother and he were very close. We all went to the station to meet them and visit for a while. They brought Anna and I a lot of chocolate Easter eggs and rabbits wrapped in gold and silver foil, prettier than any I'd ever seen before. One extra-large rabbit had a basket on his back which was filled with bonbons. It aged on my windowsill, as it was too pretty and rare for me to eat.

Anton did not flee when all the Germans did. He and his wife had three lovely daughters and a loving Croatian family. He thought that loyalty was enough to keep him safe, as he had never shown prejudice towards Yugoslavian people. But he was wrong. He was put in prison for false war crimes committed against Serbians. They were all trumped up charges. He was a prisoner of the Tito regime for many years doing hard labor. He came out a broken man. He found us many years later in New York through the Red Cross, as he wondered how my mother and her family fared through all this turmoil.

Mom's mother's name was Katharina Gartner, and she lived in central Serbia where her father was a land owner. Rich land owners in the heart of Serbia preferred to marry their daughters off to German men, if at all possible, to get them out of central Serbia and into the German-speaking region of Yugoslavia that was more industrial. While her maternal grandfather never looked for my mother as a child, we as family—shortly after my sister Anna was born—sought out the family farm, which my mother inherited from her mother it was said. We went by train and walked far, with my father carrying Anna on his back, to seek out the farm. We received down pillows and bed covers from my mother's grandfather Gartner, and nothing else. We carried this back home to Indjija and took them to America. The old duvet was cleaned and altered for me when I got married to Lorenz Buschbacher in 1954. When the extension of the house in Indjija was finished circa 1936/37, my parents set up beds for me and Anna to make a special bedroom. I remember on this trip, I was scared walking for so long, and it was cold and drizzling. There were no friendly people in sight. We were hungry and tired; nobody spoke German there. It was mostly farm land. My father stopped passing wagons with farm workers to ask for directions to the Gartner family farm. People knew who they were and where the farm was. We followed their direction. We finally arrived at a massive wooden gate. My father left us there, while he went to another house to tell them who we were, and to ask the Gartners to let us in. I remember a short elderly person opening the gate and crying because she could not hear us pounding at the gate, and she could not talk to us. She was deaf; she hugged my mother so tightly that I got scared she would harm her. She cried and cried. To this day, I don't know how she was related to my mother. In this household, nobody spoke German, but the father of my grandmother. There were a lot of people who tended to Anna and me, but we did not know what they said to us. We left as soon as possible, maybe even the next day, with only the down duvet and pillows they gave us. Life was different back then in my grandmother's house. Her father raised her and sent her off on her own, never to look back. He never helped my mother, his grandchild, when she was left alone with her father his daughter died. But of course, we all want to know where we came from, and we still want to know what became of our homes.

Our schooling in Indjija lasted six years, from age 6 to 12. We attended *Volkschule* (elementary school) for four years, then Bürgerschule for two more years. Then, we were expected to become an apprentice to learn a trade (even a shop attendant required an apprenticeship), or to go to work on a farm or factory. Few students were rich enough to go to Belgrade or Zagreb to study. Education in Indjija was in German, and university courses were taught in Serbian, Croatian, depending in which city you lived in; Belgrade, Serbia or Zagreb, Croatia. Working with your hands was more encouraged. If you did not have a trade, it was hard to have steady employment. Boys had many opportunities to learn a trade at 12 years old. They signed on as an apprentice with a master in a given profession, for which the family paid. Girls were expected to marry, raise a family, and run a household. The lucky ones worked in the retail stores. Even there, you became an apprentice to learn the retail business, such as shoe sales in a shoe store, pharmaceuticals in the drug store, or menswear in a haberdashery. Working as a seamstress was a favorite, as the girls learned to sew from their mothers at an early age. As an apprentice, you went to night school for more education. It was called *Lehrbuben* (apprentice) school.

On my street lived a young lady named, Apolonia. I loved her name as it was different from most of the girls I knew—just like mine, many of theirs were Catholic saint's names. Apolonia worked in the drug store, and when she went home after work she smelled of perfume. She wore her white shop coat home often, and we girls who played on the street were in awe of her. She was beautiful and smelled so fine we all wanted to be like her. Of course, like all other neighbors, I never saw her or heard anything about her after we left home in 1944. Every family escaped the best way they could for their own safety, and could not take the time to care how others managed to get out. I hope Apolonia fared well, and had a long and happy life.

Family farming was the major occupation. Most Yugoslavians lived off the land, especially in the Danube region, which was extremely fertile. The Nazis occupied the area for so long because, when they came to Yugoslavia in 1942, it was like opening a vault of food and manpower. It gave them a boost to continue their quest.

The Austrian Empire was no more, but Austrians living in the Balkan region of Yugoslavia and Hungary were considered Germans, as Austria was annexed to Germany in the beginning of the war. German-speaking people of Poland, Czechoslovakia, Romania, and Hungary were also considered Germans. Their countries later allowed displaced persons from their region to return home after the war, but Tito refused. He had his own brand of Communism, not to the liking of Stalin, the Russian leader. Tito shut down two unarmed US planes, I heard. By 1944, the Soviet Army had advanced deep into the heart of Eastern Europe, and with it Soviet political agents formed the basis for Communist control in Yugoslavia. Titoism took hold.

While the Communist Party was outlawed in Yugoslavia before, now it was growing underground. The greatest organizer was a machinist named, Josip Broz. He was a Croatian, who fought in the Austro-Hungarian Army during World War I, during which he was captured and imprisoned in Russia. There, he was indoctrinated in Communism. After the Russian Revolution, he started plotting how to get rid of the Germans. He had been thoroughly trained in Communist subversive tactics. In 1937, he became the

Chief of the Communist Movement and was called "Marshal Tito." He began organizing under cover. In his island home, he plotted how to get rid of Germans in Yugoslavia. His movement was secretive; one could not identify the local partisans. Their leaders came from other parts of Yugoslavia to our region. They hid in the wheat fields all around German towns, raiding outlying farms, raping and killing inhabitants. I personally witnessed a young farmer return home from his field, draped over his horse in grave pain, and barely alive. The flesh on his back was mutilated, carved with Swastikas and salt poured into his wounds. A note was pinned to his flesh that read, "Germans get out."

As the months turned to years, the raids on German families increased to the point that all German men (including my father) still at home were given guns and sent out to patrol the perimeter of Indjija every night It was not safe for us to live there anymore, because the surrounding wheat fields were full of Tito's partisans. I was 11 years old at the time. My family lived in the home on Lastina Uliza number 9 since 1928 with the same wonderful neighbors. It was as hard to see these bad things happening to them, as it was to family members.

In the meantime, my father was busy protecting what we had to leave behind for later, and prepared necessities for our eventual escape. He made a crate for bedding and packed clothes for traveling, while my grandfather built a wall to cover the front of the connecting wall in between my parent's bedroom and the guest room. The new wall created a secret space to hide our own favorite linens, towels, China, and other household goods. We had a concrete cistern to collect rain water from the roof of the house. It had been raining, so it was full. As we were leaving, my mother dropped her enamel cook wear into the cistern to hide it from the partisans, who were waiting to get into our houses. It was

actually the perfect weather for such
a happening. In 1988, my parents, as
American citizens visited Indjija and
were asked by the new homeowners to
come into what once was their house.
My mother saw her enamel coffee pot
on the stove. She cried, and the lady
said these pots had just been found,
as the rainwater shielded them in the
cistern. But the current owners never
saw the fake wall in the bedroom, or
any other items of my parents. They
had bought the house from the former
partisan owners, that occupied it when
we left in 1944.

Family Bachert, Last
remembrance of home
Indjija, 1944

In autumn 1944, the farmers could not harvest wheat or pick
grapes, because it was not possible to leave the safety of the patrolled town without being shot, beheaded, or otherwise harmed
by the partisans outside. The caretakers of these farms and vineyards were killed or enslaved by the partisans, who took over.

We always slaughtered two or three pigs at this time of year to
smoke meat and make sausages to feed us for the winter. This
year, our family, with the help of a neighboring butcher, did this
a little earlier, so as to have the ham and sausage ready by the
time we had to leave. The family hoped to take enough food to
last till the war's end, when we could come back home again.

In October 1944, we were ready and eager to get out of town.
But since the railroad station had been bombed, there was no
track for a train to get us out. Later, it became possible to use the
old railroad station for people to leave from Indjija. We were not

farmers, and we had no horse or wagon. But soon, a neighboring farmer generously offered us a horse and wagon, if we would take his elderly parents to safety with us. He could not leave his animals without anybody tending to them—his cows had to be milked every day by hand. Our grandfather handled the horses, and invited the farmer's parents to ride with us to the city of Ruma. Dad stayed behind safeguarding the town. That wagon was a godsend, as otherwise we would have had to wait until someone else was willing to take us with them.

The men on patrol stayed active and alert at the edges of town until all the women and children were safely delivered. It was a day's travel from our beloved Indjija. I remember kissing Dad goodbye. My mom opened the pens and stalls to let the animals fend for themselves, as nobody would feed them now. She said goodbye to all of them as she loved them, especially Emma the goat. We were all crying, as we said goodbye to the animals. They must have wondered what was happening, because they, too, seemed sad and listless. They never came to the front yard, let alone the street. How confusing it all was for man and beast. My most vivid memory of that day was remembering our dog, Laura, wanting desperately to get on the wagon with us. She was a black and white hound, who was very smart and lovable. But, she was getting old. I had known her all my life and I was 12 years old, and Laura

Goat Emma, Maria Bachert, Last hug at home
Lastina Ulica, Indjija, 1944

was as old, or older. She couldn't go with us where we were going, into the unknown. My father gave her a whistle, and she ran to the back yard to him. We heard a shot, and then a dead quiet fell over all of us. Opa gave a tug on the reigns, the horses ran, and off we went to Ruma; into the unfamiliar world ahead.

Later, it started to rain hard. We were cold, hungry, and wet; besides being frightened of possible attacks by partisans along the muddy, rain-soaked road. The trip to Ruma took much longer than usual in these conditions. There was a caravan of wagons from Indjija to Ruma that day, but nobody that I knew.

We sat on that wagon, bumping down the rut of a road in the rain for many hours until we reached Ruma safely. We were expected there. Cots were prepared in a local school auditorium for all who came that night. Supper was cooked by the ladies that helped us get settled. We washed up and put on dry clothes. Finally, we went to sleep and waited for the train ride in the morning. As I fell asleep, I missed my Dad, but my dog most of all, and as I prayed my evening prayer, I could only think of Laura. We had our dolly, Kristl. She had a friendly ceramic face with blue eyes, that reminded me of the cornflowers in the meadow where Anna and I played. I was told I was too old for dolls at age 12, but Anna let me hug her too. We three shared the bed; it was comforting to have Anna and Kristl to sleep with that night. I felt a little safer now, as our neighbors were making us very comfortable in the auditorium. We did not wait too long, maybe a day, for a train to come and take us to a safe place till the war ended, and we could return to our home.

Ruma was just a stop to get us to another safe place. We waited only a day or two before a train came to take us out of this troubled land. With partisans crawling in the wheat fields and the

Red Army within earshot, we were in a hurry to leave. When we boarded the train, every precious thing was taken from us, and thrown away. My doll and Anna's doll carriage are the things that come to mind right now. People said there was no room for frivolous things like children's dolls, or even a violin. We thought the train was taking us to Germany. We did not know where we were going, it just was important to get away from In-djija. Somehow, we had to let Dad know where to find us, when he was cleared to leave.

We were on that train for days and days. As we went through Hungary, that lonely airplane—the one which unloaded the black eggs on our train station—found us again. Suddenly, the train stopped, and we were all running into the woods next to the train tracks to take cover from the bullets directed at us. We were only a bunch of women and children! Imagine that. What kind of a fearful enemy were we? I remember my grandfather carrying four-year-old Anna on his shoulders as we ran. Anna's shoe fell off, but grandfather would not stop to pick it up. She cried, but grandfather told her it was alright to lose a shoe. She is too young to die. We safely got out of that mess and back to the train to continue our escape. When we got back on the train, I saw a bullet hole in the sleeve of a coat that was left hanging by the window seat. Thank God nobody was wearing it at the time.

As we reached Austria, another obstacle befell us. The track our train was traveling on was partly blown up. Somehow, we managed to get to a safe destination in Austria. Oberösterreich, near St. Polten. We were taken off the train, and escorted to housing all around the village, wherever there was room. We were lucky to get a caretaker's house in the yard of an apartment complex. It was private, and we were comfortable. We had food from home that my mother cooked for us.

The Final Good Bye to Indjija, Our Home for Five Generations, Came on November 11, 1944

Dad and the men who were left to make sure Tito's partisans didn't over run the town, gathered up the hungry, crying animals, roaming through town, and filled a freight train to send them to Germany for food. I imagine that even the animals were confused, as to what happened to their lives. I feel sorry for my Emma, the milk-giving goat for all my life on earth up to that time, who never left our yard. The men used the horses left to make a transport for themselves to evacuate. There were a few families left that did not want to leave their possessions, and had no fear of another regime coming in to govern the country. But they now decided to go also.

Indjija was a ghost town with hungry animals roaming through the streets and no one left to feed them. These people had lived under the Austro/Hungarian Empire and the Yugoslavian Kingdom. They managed fine then, and they would adjust now too, they thought. But the hateful Titoists had other ideas; they threw them into prison, forced them to work on the pig farms outside of town, or even killed them.

In 1996, Valentin Oberkersch wrote a book called, *India Deutsches Leben in Ost Syrmien*, about our town. He wrote about how the first Germans arrived in Indjija in 1825. My family name Bachert appears in1833, when Stefan Bachert and wife Katharina Stadler came from a nearby Hungarian town called Prestovatz, which is now in an Austrian region called Banat.

ॐ

Chapter Four

Landing in Upper Austria, near St. Polten (Fall/Winter 1944)

After panting and waiting for what seemed like forever, our rescuers had dug a hole through some safe-enough spot to pull us out one by one. The rush of fresh, dusty air into what we thought might be our grave, was so welcome and so calming.

A few weeks after arriving, I went to school and made friends with a girl in my class, who lived in an apartment near where we lived in a caretaker's cottage. She was nice, and she had a brown shirt uniform, which she wore to school on certain days, as did most of the girls in class. I wanted a brown shirt too, but we did not know where to get one. I asked to borrow it to take my picture. She kindly loaned it to me, but I don't know if I ever got a picture, as we did not stay there very long, just through the winter.

Teachers soon discovered that I could not read the blackboard and needed glasses. We were sent to an eye doctor in St. Polten, I remember my visit to the eye doctor, who gave me the first of many pairs of glasses, which I would need throughout my life. But he wanted to do more tests and called me back to his office the following week.

What made the next visit to the eye doctor so memorable was a series of events that marked that day in the war for me. He wanted to examine the back of my eyes using a new procedure, which I had never experienced before. He put drops in both of my eyes to dilate them, which we now know is common practice. We arrived at the doctor's office in mid-morning after an uncomfortable train ride. Mother and I did not know that mid-morning was becoming a regular time for air raids over the city. I was sitting patiently, waiting for the eye drops to work, when the air-raid siren screamed. Immediately, the office closed and we all ran for shelter under the street. It was disorienting, because my vision was blurry and everything was too bright, but my mother led me to a safe place. The air-raid shelter was at the end of the street, which was about a block long. We quickly followed all the other people, who knew where they were going. They descended into the ground through a heavy door into a dark and strange place, lit by a single lightbulb in the hall, dangling from the ceiling.

In the small, dank room where the crowd of strangers gathered, there were benches against a wall where Mom and I sat down. Some of the people with us had experienced this before and told us not to worry. They said it would be over soon, and we could get back to what we were doing. Others were prepared and had brought snacks to eat, as if we'd be there for some time. Some prayed out loud, but most of us sat there quietly, deep in our own thoughts. I looked around and began to wonder what to make of this, and why were we there at all since nothing had happened since the air-raid siren blasted?

Soon, I learned why everyone scurried from their homes and businesses to take shelter underground. I heard the explosions of bombs so close, that they made the earth shake. Such noises I had never heard before. The light bulb went out in the hallway, and someone lit dim lanterns in the main room. The entrance where we came in was suddenly filled with rubble, and our safe place became even more dark and frightening. Mom held me tight and said, "Don't worry, it will be okay." I trusted her, so I sat quietly holding on to her words, and hugged her body. She took out her Catholic rosary and told me to pray with her. We prayed for so long that I had no idea how much time had passed. It could have been a few minutes, or an hour. I could hear people nearby softly crying, or singing, or praying. A few of the women screamed and fainted, and it terrified me. The air was thick with dust. It was hot, stuffy, and hard to breath. Finally, the booming from the bombs stopped, and the earth stopped shaking. Soon after, the siren sounded the *all clear*, but we could not get out.

People tried to push the rubble away to no avail. The harder they tried, the more they kept falling down under the weight of the thick air, and the heavy rubble. Our exit was buried under a fallen building, and we were trapped in this dungeon for what seemed an eternity. The air was getting scarcer which created more panic, which in turn reduced the air for the rest of us. Some people became so overwhelmed with fear that they got louder and louder. The screaming, crying, and fainting continued until there were just a few of us gulping down the last of the fresh air, giving us precious minutes of hope to be rescued. Mom and I continued to quietly pray, and pray. This went on for probably hours. By then, it was quieter, as most of those who had fainted were asleep; some mumbling in their dreams, or some state of semi-consciousness.

What broke the monotony of the dread was someone saying they heard bulldozers digging above us. What a welcome sound that would be! We all went quiet, and listened to hear if it was true. It was! After panting and waiting for what seemed like forever, our rescuers had dug a hole through some safe-enough spot at the other end of this dungeon to pull us out one by one. The rush of fresh, dusty air into what we thought might be our grave, was so welcome, and so calming. The rescue workers were kind and helpful. With the uniformed professionals were Red Cross volunteers, woman with doughnuts, drinks, and water to wipe away the dust. It was plain to see these people did this before, and were well trained to bring calm professionalism to a triage area. Those who were able were free to leave, as my mother and I did, as quickly as possible. We were in a different street now, but we did find our way to the train station to catch the next train out of St. Polten, never to return. It was dusk and we realized we had been there a very long time, as we did not have a watch. We hoped we would be getting a train home soon.

Before anything else might happen, Mom and I took the train home to our little garden shed, in a small town, where we felt safe to wait out the war. I never knew the name of this town, but we were there through the winter of 1945. We had brought food from home; when we left we had a whole pig in barrels under lard and salt cure to last a long while. We also had smoked sausage, which Dad and Opa made. We were never so thankful to see our family again, as we were that evening. Mom and I ran into the garden shed. By then it was late at night. We were not even hungry, just overcome with feelings that were new to me.

For now, my mother said, we would not go back to the eye doctor in St Polten. And I was just fine with the glasses I had.

Anna was six years old, the age for Catholic children to celebrate their First Holy Communion. It was something we'd been looking forward to along with my Confirmation ceremony. But in this part of Austria, at this time, church-going was not encouraged. We were grateful for the life we had, and so we did not complain about ceremonies. We had food to eat from home. My Dad had found us, I had friends, and I liked school. The only time I felt out of place was when all the girls in class had their brown shirt uniforms on, and I did not. But they never teased me about it, or bullied me in any way. I was happy there. We never went to church since leaving our home town. My mother said that I would be confirmed when we got back home to Yugoslavia, and Anna would get her First Holy Communion then too, and all would be as it was before the war began.

When my father had found us, it was nearly Christmas 1944, and that was a gift for us all. He found us by word of mouth from other people, who were on the train with us. He, and the other men that stayed behind, were the last transport leaving Indjija, on November 7, 1944. They had a more dangerous time then we did. The German Army got desperate; they needed help. They stopped the transport on a bridge, and went through the wagons taking food and rifles, and even some of the younger men as well. Luckily, the transport leader was able to connect with a German Army general, who reprimanded his men and ordered them to let the wagons pass over the bridge into Hungary. In Hungary, they found some kind people with farms on the outskirts of town, where they could let the horses rest. Other times, they had to take hay they saw in fields without permission. The important thing was, we found each other, and were united as a family again.

Mom exchanged pork meat for things that we needed with some people who lived in the apartment house. The Austrians had not seen so much meat in years. They were very grateful. I remember some Serbian men came to see us. They heard we were from Yugoslavia. They were so glad to hear about their homeland, and to speak their language with my parents, and grandfather. My mother gave them my report card. It was in Serbian with pictures of our kings; King Alexander, his son, Peter, and others that I did not know. They were happy to get it, as they were away from home a long time. I think they must have been Nazis prisoners. They just wanted to get back home.

My father found us only through the grace of God. After two months, we still had some food from home, and were doing well in the comfortable gardener's cottage. We were planning to stay only long enough to wait out the war. Little did we know that Russia's Red Army was close to Vienna, and not far from us. We had to flee again.

I was 12 years old and my sister, Anna, was six, my brother was not yet born. Our new, peaceful life was shattered again. Soon, we would be in harm's way again. What to do now? My grandfather advised us to get out because the Russians had a reputation for cruelty, especially to women. He said to my parents, "You are young and have a family to protect. Your husband is here now, so go in God's name. I am too old to run any longer, and I will stay here. I can speak Serbian, and I will get along with the Russians, I will stay right here, I'll be alright."

CR

Chapter Five

Fleeing Again: Becoming Hobos
(Early Spring 1945)

We dropped to the ground just in time to feel the dirt cover us when the bullets hit the ground next to our bodies. Only by the grace of God were we not killed.

We left grandfather the rest of the food we had, made ourselves a picnic basket, and went on our way with just the clothes on our backs. It was getting warmer now, as it was early spring 1945. We walked south, as that is all we knew to get further away from the approaching Red Army. Farther south, we were sure, we would be safer. We came to a working train yard, where we stowed away on a freight train going south as far as we could. After a day or two, the train stopped for good in a large, abandoned terminal. Many trains were standing there; some rusty, some better looking. We did not know where we were, but it looked okay for the moment. We just knew we were far away from Oberösterreich and the troubles there.

My father set out to look for lodging for us. We waited for him in this abandoned station for a long and boring day. Anna and I decided to go outside, to run and play among the abandoned freight trains. Coal dust was flying up at us, and we saw that the dusty earth was riddled with shell craters. Then, we heard it. That lonely Russian plane had found us again. Anna and I listened to the roar of its engine, and, looking up, we saw it heading straight for us. Our mother screamed to us from the doorway of the station house, "Lie down! Lie down right now!" We dropped to the ground just in time to feel the dirt cover us when the bullets hit the ground next to our bodies. Only by the grace of God were we not killed. Our faces buried in the coal dust, stunned by what just happened, we were frozen to the ground. Clearly, playtime was over. It was okay to wait inside, as it was getting to be dusk anyway. We were in shock, just sitting silently. Mom brushed the dust off us and took out her rosary to pray. I could feel her heart pumping, as she hugged me, crying. We were tired and hungry, and just exhausted by life itself. Childhood should be fun.

After what seemed like forever, we saw our father again. He had bread for us, and good news. He got a job on a mountain top farm, whose men had been called to the *Volkssturm* (a national militia established by Nazi Germany). The farmer's wife and daughter needed help farming. This was good news for us, as we would have food to eat on a farm. It took us most of the next day to get to this farm high up the mountain. I was amazed that my father found the way to get there again, and wondered how he had found this place to begin with. The two farmer ladies were friendly and welcoming. Dinner was ready when we arrived, and we were invited to sit with them to eat. We held hands to say grace. We felt safe once again. Dinner was a pan full of roasted potatoes, and a bowl of buttermilk. Everyone had a spoon with which to eat from the single bowl of milk and potatoes on the table. It was strange for us to eat this way, but grateful to have food. Mom asked the ladies if she could have some items to cook for us separately, as we had a caretaker's cottage across from the farmhouse all to ourselves, which was wonderful. They were happy about this too, as they did not have to worry about "Franz's children." My dad's name was Franz and that's what they called us.

ખ

Chapter Six

The Grandeur of the Tirolean Mountain Top (1945)

It was a picturesque place full of the natural beauty of wildflowers, grass, and trees, as far as the eye could see.

The farm was located in Tirol, the southernmost part of Austria. The region just over the mountains is now known as Bavaria, Germany. I don't know the name of the small town in the valley. We could see it, but we never went down. We were simply glad to be in a secluded place, filled with peace and quiet. The people in southern Germany and Austria greet you by saying "Grüss Gott," (originally meaning God bless you). Tiroleans are very Catholic; wooden carvings of the Stations of the Cross are placed along the routes up to the mountains. The hiking trails on the mountain are clean and pretty. I could picture the young people in better times going up and down these mountains singing a yodel or two, while the older people said the rosary.

The farmers gave us flour and other food items they could spare, and Mom would cook for us. We were again in a lovely garden hut, comfortable and safe, for the most part. It was a picturesque place full of the natural beauty of wildflowers, grass, and trees, as far as the eye could see. This was still spring of 1945. The cornflowers were blooming and other wildflowers showed their happy faces, their color ready to burst into bloom any day. It was a tranquil place, except for the droning of the bomb-laden planes, passing overhead every day at the same time. They looked heavy, flying slowly over the mountains from Germany. They shone so bright in the sun, they looked like they were made from pure silver. They flew in a perfectly symmetrical formation. There was a certain beauty in this whole thing, and I admired it. Never had I seen shiny planes of that size—only that lonely Russian Mig pursuing us. It was ugly and black, like stale smoke. I tried to count these beautiful shiny planes, but there were too many, I never could count them all. I did not know where they were going; I was only glad they did not unload their cargo on us. I quickly shook off that vision in my head of a rubble-laden bunker, with fainting people.

Dad's new job on the farm was wonderful. The two ladies on the farm were very nice and glad they had a man to help them. Mom cleaned the stone building and made it *home*. It sat across the street from the main farm house, in a meadow nestled in the forest. The view was wonderful, nature at its best. We had an outhouse nearby, and lots of room to run and chase butterflies. There were two more houses along the dirt road, but I don't know who lived there. They would have been only woman and children, I am sure, as the men, no matter what age, were sent to fight as Volksturm, in a last-ditch effort to save the war.

Mom cleared a patch of land for a vegetable garden. Dad worked in the field along with the two women, but he left the milking of the cows to them, as it had to be done by hand every evening. His pay was milk, eggs, flour, potatoes, etc. We lived well and happily.

One day, while Mom was planting her garden, a German soldier came out of the woods. He was very young, of a slight build, and he had a dog with him. He befriended us, and let us play with his dog. He told us that the German Army was training dogs in the woods nearby. But, I never heard any barking, or saw other soldiers, so I don't know where he came from, or why. He seemed always to come out of the woods, when we were playing outside and Mom was working in the garden. I felt like he was watching us, and knew what we were doing at all times; it made me uneasy. I did not like this man. I think his name was Wolfgang. He wanted to be friends with us, and Mom was happy to talk to another adult for a while. Anna and I liked his dog.

One time, after he had visited us several times, I found myself alone playing in the grass with his dog, when his hands touched my private parts. This shocked me cold, he smiled at me and held me down with his other hand on my shoulder. I did not know how his hand made it up my dress without me noticing it. I was startled, and did not know what to do. It did not go any further, and I was glad when he left quickly with his dog. I was afraid to tell my mother. From then on, I was very cautious to watch the edge of the woods when we went outside. When I saw him coming, I ran and locked myself in the outhouse until he was gone. My mother enjoyed talking to him, as it was often the only adult conversation she had for days. Anna enjoyed petting his dog, but I was afraid of this man. Luckily, it was not long before he was gone for good. The roar of the silver planes came to an end, as well. The mountain top in Tirol became tranquil again.

There is a song I remember that goes like this, *"Der Liebe Gott muss ein Tiroler sein, weil er schenkt uns nur den besten Wein."* It means, "God must be a Tiroler because he grants us the best wine." There is some truth in this. I know.

CR

Chapter Seven

The War is Over! (1945)

It was a nice time on the Tirolian Mountain top,
and it came to an end too soon.

Summer was approaching and the grass was getting high, full of clover and buttercups. It was a beautiful time of year. We never went to church, it was too far down the mountain, and too hard to come back up. On Sundays, the locals dressed in their native costume to go down the mountain to church. They wore Dirndls, which are full, gathered, black skirts, colorful vests, and white blouses with puffy sleeves, and an apron of silk in a contrasting color. The ladies also wore a black hat. The men wore Leder-hosen, which are over-the-knee pants, not the short Lederhosen worn in Bavaria. These leather pants, with handsome, colorful, wool design stitching, are tightened at the calf, with little calf-warmers knitted in white with colorful stripes on top and bottom, above the shoe. The outfit is completed with red or green shirts, hats, and matching leather jackets.

When the locals came back one Sunday in May 1945, they said American soldiers are in town, and that the war is over. THE WAR IS OVER!! We shouted in glee! We thought we could go back home to our little town of Indjija, and forget this part of our life forever. But no, it was not to be. Soon, a truckload of American soldiers came to live in the farm house, where the mother and daughter were. They were to observe and catch fleeing German soldiers, when they came over the mountains from Germany. It was a boring job, as nobody came.

The American soldiers played cards, laughed, and smoked cigarettes. They were friendly and happy it was all over. Some were of German ancestry, or had wives who were. They showed us pictures of their family. They were looking forward to going home to them very soon.. There was a young soldier, who spent his time with us. He did not like playing cards. Instead, he drew pictures of things, and told us the names of these items in English, and I told him the German name for each one. It was fun to learn from him. He had a talent for art, which I loved. We took nature walks and learned from each other. He traded his rations with us in return for a meal of bean soup and noodles, which my mother made. Anna and I ate the food he shared, which was delivered every noontime by truck. He watched my mother make her own noodles, as we could not buy anything prepared in Austria. Everybody made their own noodles, strudels, and bread. David was our American friend's name. He said in America nobody makes noodles from scratch, but it reminded him of his grandmother, who always made meals from scratch. Again, it was too short a time for fun, as he soon left with his troop to go home. I hope he had a nice long life. He enjoyed our cooking, and we enjoyed his rations. They had meat in them every day, which Anna and I enjoyed eating, as we lived mainly on vegetables. We especially liked the canned peaches for desert. It was a nice time on the Tirolean mountain top, and it came to an end too soon. The American soldiers left. I hope they got to go home. Now, French soldiers came by to round up all the refugees.

CR

Chapter Eight

Kufstein, Austria:
DP Camp (1945)

One night, we got up and ran through the woods nearby.
Once out of sight, we slowed to walking in the dark.
It was frightening to me.
Suddenly, we heard shouts of, "Halt! Stehen bleiben."

By the autumn 1945, the Allied Forces split Austria between them into three parts. Russians occupied Oberösterreich, where we left our grandfather. Central Austria belonged to the Americans, and the southern area, where we were, was given to the French. The French forces rounded up all who were not native Austrians, and we were on the move again.

We were placed into barracks at what became a Displaced Person's (DP) Camp in Kufstein. It had previously served as hous-

ing for Polish forced laborers under Hitler. They were now pa-
trolling the outer perimeter of the camp, as they were free and
awaiting transport back home. The camp was located in a valley
in a majestic mountain range. It was an unnatural scar marring
the beauty of that natural place.

There were 64 people in our room. We were kept under lock and
key, and under careful observation, especially at night. Our room
had wall-to-wall bunk beds with a horse blanket, and a dirty pil-
low for each of us. Mom and Dad shared the bottom bunk, and
Anna and I slept on the top. Next to us was a young widow, with
a son about eight years old. Her husband was taken into the German Army from Yugoslavia. She did not know his whereabouts,
or even if he was alive. Another family of older parents, with an
adult daughter and a three-year-old grandchild, were also near
us. The daughter's husband was in the war somewhere, also con-
scripted into service from Yugoslavia. The little three-year-old
girl befriended everyone. She liked to sing and play with the
adults, and was a breath of fresh air for us all. People slept in
their clothes, as there was no privacy. My parents and the widow
hung a blanket to make a curtain between their two beds. Mom
put kerosene on our heads at night to kill the lice from the dirty
pillows.

Outside, nearby was a bathhouse with many showers, but no
doors for privacy. Mom asked me to stand in front of the stall,
and hold a towel to hide her while she showered. We also did this
when we had to use the toilet. You could feel how uncomfortable
everyone was. The United Nations Relief and Rehabilitation Ad-
ministration (UNRRA) truck came every day to bring us food.
We were rationed two slices of bread with one slice of meat for
supper, and a bowl of soup for lunch. It was very simple, terrible food to satisfy our hunger. It wasn't a time to be choosey.

I can tell you my mother made better soup with field greens, half-spoilt onions, and potatoes, which we found in the garbage dump.

At night, the French soldiers raided the barracks, looking under beds for escaping German soldiers we might be harboring. I can only assume they were looking for stragglers, who slipped past the Poles at the perimeter and came in to hide. They also took girls from our barracks to their headquarters at night, and it was terrifying. I vividly remember one time when all was quiet, the single lightbulb on the ceiling being turned on, accompanied by shouting. A group of French soldiers rushed into the room with bayonets attached to their rifles. They looked as though they were ready to attack a battalion of armed, enemy soldiers. One soldier charged at my bed, with his bayonet he raised my blanket off, and pushed me to get up. I was scared, and did as he said. My mother knew what he wanted. Without thought of her own safety, she jumped up and shielded me from him. I was surprised to hear her cry out and then speak in French to him. To my surprise and great relief, the soldier pushed me back down onto my bed, and went on to a bed, where there was an older girl. Luckily, my mother remembered enough French from when she was a domestic servant in France, and she shamed him into leaving me alone. I was only 13 years old. She also pointed him in the direction of a young woman much older than me. That lady's name was Rosa. From then on, every night a French Army officer's chauffeur came to pick her up for a party at their headquarters, which was in Castle Kufstein on a mountain top. She sometimes brought us kids gifts of chocolate candy, which for us was rarer than gold. She slept most of the day, and did not mingle much with others. We all knew she did what she had to do to survive. My mother was particularly grateful to Rosa, because she saved me from that terrible experience.

Winter was in fine form, as we saw the beautiful white snow Austria is famous for cover the ground to a pristine white. But, we did not go outside except to wait for the UNRRA truck every day. We also had no clothing to warm us in this weather. We were warm enough in the barracks, and the nightly French raids had stopped. Most of the Polish men had been taken home, and things were quiet now. We often thought of that stone cottage on the Tirol mountain top and wondered if we would be warm there. Or if they even would have kept us on in winter, when there was no work on the farm for my father to do. We hoped they picked and ate the carrots and cabbage planted in that little patch of soil where my mother worked so hard.

Soon, it was Christmas, or so they said. Every day was the same routine for us, waiting for the UNRRA truck to bring us soup that looked like mortar, and tasted like it too. Somehow, a lit-

Maria, Franz Bachert, Regina Schneider Kider, Käthe Bachert, Seppi Schneider, Anna Bachert, Lager Kufstein Christmas, 1945

tle fir tree appeared in our room to remind us of Christmas. One family had cotton balls, and we picked them apart to make snow on this little Christmas tree. It looked pretty and served as a peaceful reminder of a time gone by.

The future looked so bad for us that some people were compelled to run away at night. With the heavy patrols diminished to a handful of French troops, these brave souls ran through the woods, and across the border to Germany. We heard they were more hospitable to displaced persons of German heritage and did not keep them in prison camps. A few people were successful in escaping. It became a big discussion in our room. Dad said No to the idea, and my Mom said yes. And so, it was decided when another group of escapees were getting ready to leave, Mom and I would go with them. Dad and Anna would stay behind and wait for us to send for them. One night, we got up and ran through the woods nearby. Once out of sight, we slowed to a walk. It was frightening for me. Suddenly, we heard shouts of, *"Halt! Stehen bleiben."* (Stop! Stand still.) We all froze and did not move. It was a military patrol, and to this day I don't know if they were German, or Austrian. Either way, they knew we were from the camp, and put us in jail overnight with a warning. The next morning, they put us on a truck, and gave us back to the French authorities. It seemed the border patrol was strengthened by then, because so many had successfully escaped before us. Dad was glad to see us safe, and yet out of fear he told my mother, "You and your dumb ideas caused shame for all of us."

By now, about 18 months had passed, and most kids had lost one or two years of education. The grown-ups tried to teach us, but with no books, or even paper and pencils, it did not go very well. I do remember one thing: I loved the lady who taught us the native dances of Yugoslavia and Hungary. I also loved to sing. That was the entirety of my education. Next, a law was passed that the displaced children had to be taken in at the local school. A bus came to take us to a school in a nearby town, though I don't know what it was called. It may have been Imst. We were greeted with a pummeling of snowballs from the students there and shouts of, "Gypsies go home!" I lost my eye glasses when an icy-hard snowball hit my face. When I found them, the frame was broken. These were the glasses, which nearly cost me my life in St. Polten. The teachers did not know what to do with us, once we managed to get inside. They did not want us to mix with their children, understandably, as they assumed we were ridden with head lice. But our mothers put gasoline on our heads regularly to prevent that from happening. As uncomfortable as the shower stalls were, we still showered and cleaned ourselves every day and washed our clothes there also. I think the Tirolean school system was at a loss of what to do with us we had lost at least one or more years of schooling. Eventually, the teachers put us up in the auditorium all day, and taught us Tirolean history and songs. Still no books, but I guess they did not have many for their own children, and certainly none for us. My sister and I always sang these songs, while doing dishes when lived in Anif, later in life. As with so many things, this too did not last very long, as our family was transferred to another town, and another camp, around March 1946. It is amazing how many forced labor camps there were in the woods of Austria. I have no idea what all those prisoners labored at day after day.

ᴄᴚ

Chapter Nine

Transfer to Lager Haiming (1946 to 1947)

Friendship was very tight and loyal in Lager Haiming.
I have my scrapbook still, and I often think of this nice place,
filled with hopes and dreams for so many of us.

We were greeted in Haiming on more friendly terms. It was now spring 1946. Mother Nature dressed up to welcome us with green mountains all around this large row of barracks in the valley. This was yet another former German Army forced labor camp for men.

We were given a room to ourselves, as was every other family that came, and that was a welcome relief. There were brooms and other equipment to clean and make it livable. We had a communal kitchen where residents cooked for us, and got extra food in pay. They also created a school building, where we were able to go three hours per day per age, two or three age groups at a time.

Far right end, Käthe Bachert, Choir practice
Volksdeutches Lager Haiming Tirol, 1946

It was known that all children as displaced persons had lost several years of schooling. The teachers were people from our homeland, who lived there. They, too, were paid in extra food. A teacher in a neighboring school saw our boys at the fence watching the Austrian kids play soccer. That kind teacher gave our teacher a soccer ball. The French camp director soon saw to it that there was space for a playground and a soccer field created for us. A choir formed of teenagers, and I was in it. Also, clergymen came to serve communion and perform Confirmation for us. Anna was given her first communion and I was confirmed. All in all, it was a friendly comradery for both parents and children.

Käthe (13) & Anna (7) Bachert,
Confirmation & First Holy Communion,
Voksdeutches Fluchtlings Lager Haiming Tirol, 1946

Everyone worked hard to make this place as nice as it could be. They planted flowers, and kept the grounds green and tidy. It became a showcase of what a harmonious barracks community could look like. My teenage choir was invited to sing in other camps, and the boys played soccer against each other in teams. It became a competition of who, among *Volksdeutsche* DP camps, had a nicer camp in Austria. Of course, we did. *Volkdeutsches Fluchlings Lager* was the name the French gave us. German Peoples Refugee Camp. They came to the conclusion that we were former enemies, ha? This is what the United Nations Relief Organization said. So, they handed us over to the French and Austrians to feed, as UNRRA no longer did. Now I know why the French soldiers needed bayonets to raid our rooms at night in Kufstein. They thought we were going to attack them; yes, little three-year-old Susie, or my six-year-old sister Anna, what a fight they could have put up. The whole thing was absurd, but a better thing happened when they let us take care of ourselves. The Austrians provided the food based on the ration cards, and our people cooked. It was a good situation all around. Now the French government helped to provide room for a school on campus. The Austrians sent a teacher, and it became an organized existence. However, we were told we could never go back to Yugoslavia.

Little by little, family members found each other, obtained work, and moved on. This was a kind of respite for planning your future. Everyone had a dream and a vision of what was to come next. People were also coming to look for workers. My father met some men that were looking for bricklayers to take to Salzburg. It was in the American sector of Austria. That was all the encouragement my father needed to sign on with this group. He took work for a construction firm called Hoffman und Maculan. They transported us to their housing facility in the woods of Anif, between Anif and Hellbrunn, a suburb of Salzburg. It was a distance away, but the company provided transportation, so it was not a problem for my father to come and go to work. He was excited to finally be on his own to start a new life for the family. It was now winter 1947.

Recruiters came from many countries to invite us to repatriate to their country. The war had left so many people with no home to go to. In 1946/47, many countries saw an opportunity to bring refugees to their country to further cultivate rural land, and otherwise benefit the country. It also gave an opportunity to people to create a new life for themselves, and their families. I have family and friends who settled in Germany, Austria, Argentina, the USA, Canada, and Switzerland.

In Hungary, we found a cousin of my mother's family, who were on a train from Germany to Yugoslavia arranged by the Allied Forces in Germany. This was before they knew that Marshal Tito had forbidden former German/Austrian inhabitants to return to their homeland of the former Yugoslavia. He had the tracks mined, which this train was on. It was only by the grace of God Mom's cousins were spared. During the night, a kind Hungarian train worker disconnected their train car from the locomotive, while all were sleeping. In the morning, the locomotive was gone, and their car was left abandoned on the tracks in a town in Hungary called Mosh (I think). The inhabitants of this train car became Hungarians, living under Communism, and working in the fields assigned to them. His three daughters married Hungarian men, and live happily in Hungary still.

Allied Forces in Germany stopped all trains that were already organized in Stuttgart going to Yugoslavia. These refugees happily became German Citizens. It was a rude awakening for us all. Recruiters came to our camp. There were people from Australia and all of the South American countries. Chile sent a teacher, who taught us Spanish by putting everyday words to a melody we already knew. Different people chose different countries to start a new life. My father said, "If we cannot go home again, I am holding out for America." But the Americans never came to ask us to immigrate there. We actively pursued a way to apply for immigration to America, which took several years to achieve.

I had many friends; there was always a group of teens doing something nice together. We went wandering up the mountain, or cycling along the country roads. Missionaries formed these youth groups. I had friends in both Catholic and Protestant groups, and enjoyed whatever was available at the time. My favorite were the Protestants, as they asked you in your words to express gratitude to God. I had a hard time doing this, as without a prayer book I could not pray. I soon learned to look at the Nature God created, and learned to be thankful. The Catholics held Mass on the mountain top, where we received communion. It was impersonal. We all made little memory books for each other, as we knew our parents would soon decide where to settle. We had no materials to do this with, as we had no money, or even an opportunity buy anything. We found some scrap construction paper in the school room on which we drew, and created poems for a special friend to keep. We made memory books to pass around for our friends to sign. We even had a chance to take snapshots of each other. Friendship was very tight and loyal in Volksdeutsche Flutchlings Lager Haiming. I have my scrapbook still, and I often think of this happy place, filled with hopes and dreams for so many of us.

Käthe Bachert, Regina, Seppi Schneider, Celebrating Confirmation, Volksdeutches Lager Haiming Tirol, 1946

CR

Chapter Ten

Free at Last!
American Sector of Austria (Winter 1947)

*It was a rude awakening for us. We expected a normal life as
the war had been over for a while now.*

The winters in Austria are harsh and long. We did not have proper clothes to wear; no boots, Loden coats, or ski pants. It took a half hour to walk in the snow to catch the bus north to Salzburg from Anif.

The barracks owned by the construction firm Hoffman und Maculan were at the edge of Anif, in a clearing next to a river and the autobahn leading into Salzburg. Alpestrasse 8 was the mailing address, and it was home to the workers of the construction firm. The firm brought us out of the DP camp. We were now in the American Sector of Austria. From here we could apply for a visa to immigrate to America. We now were free to live a normal life.

Father had a job, the children could go to school, and mother could take care of the family. Ha! We did not know what a big surprise was in store for us.

My father got paid for his work, but we could not buy anything, not even food. The firm's two abandoned German Army barracks was on land owned by Count Johannes von Rohn de Cais, who lived up the road in a castle with a moat around it. Over the bridge was a road that led to the town of Anif, to which this land belonged. Count Johannes von Rohn de Cais owned all the forest land on both sides of the road. The only thing there was the Salzburg garbage dump, across the autobahn in the nearby forest.

At first, we were in the small barracks on the edge of the woods, facing the cleared area next to the stream, as the bigger barracks was full. In front of the outhouse was another barracks, much larger, facing the stream and the autobahn. Only farmers used the road, as very few people had cars or trucks, so it was pretty quiet. Small patches of land for gardening was available much later, when a lot of people had left after their year of duty for the firm.

There were other new people, also from Yugoslavia. There was a family nearby that my mother knew from a former camp. They had teenage sons, who also worked with their father, and a baby that my mother practically adopted. I remember crying, because I was lonely, and my mother was always preoccupied with that baby. I did not see her for most of the day. Anna spent her time there too, which left me to myself. I prayed and cried myself to sleep, as nobody cared about me. I had many friends in Lager Haiming whom I lost, just as when we left Indjija. I was depressed with no one to talk to, and nowhere to go. There were only seeing trees around me, and not even any houses were near-by. If you walked a mile to the right on the autobahn you'd get to Anif. If you walked a mile to the left, you could take a bus to Salzburg. A mile to the north was the town of Hellbrunn. To the south was a US Army camp. I was so alone.

Once, I remember staying in bed all day, because I thought I should be dying; what was the use of living this life with no pur-pose? I was alone and had no one to talk to, and I cried and cried. I prayed desperately for the salvation of my soul. Anna went to stay with Mom in the neighbor's apartment, and I was aban-doned until just before Dad came home, Mom and Anna came home to find me in bed, sobbing. There were no books to read, no radio, no boots to wear in the cold weather outside. I could, end this life with no regrets, I thought. Finally, a family moved in across the hall with a child. As I watched and waited, I saw a girl my age. It was like a flower bursting into bloom. I went to greet her, and we became best friends. They too left after her dad got finished working for Hoffman and Maculan, and I was alone again. I was 14 years old, restless for a change and some purpose to my existence. Finally, the weather warmed up, and I could go outside to walk in the park, and think.

My father made the rounds pleading with the nuns in the Catho-lic school to let me attend. It was private, so he thought he could pay tuition to get me in. I had not been in school, since we left that gardener's cottage in Oberösterreich in 1945. Since I could not go to school, I was to find work. In the forest nearby, in Hell-brunn, a perfume factory was opening soon. We girls from the barracks were excited about the opportunity to get a job so close to home! We all went for an interview together, and the man do-ing the hiring said, "I have to hire seven Austrians, before I can hire one of you." That was a blow to our enthusiasm, and we got no work there. It was the law they had to uphold.

By now, the weather was becoming nice, and the town of Anif was building a swimming pond. It was in the woods where a natural stream flowed down from the mountain. We had something new to look forward to! When at long last it was finally done, we went on a picnic, and decided to learn to swim. Low and behold, that cold water took our breath away the first second we jumped in. So, that put a damper on that great idea! The water was from the melted snow pack up on the mountain. I never did learn to swim in Austria. I taught myself at the age of 19, after we moved far away to Rockaway Beach in America. There, I had a boyfriend with a car, and we spent a lot of time on the beach together. Later in life, when I went to York College, I took swimming lessons. At the time, I also worked in Public School 63Q. At the end with an associate degree from York College, I became an Educational Associate—my final educational conquest of which I am very proud. I showed those Austrians, that I never gave up my dream of being a teacher. It took moving to America, my new home, to give me the opportunity. I was never ashamed of anything I did in my life, except when I had to fill out a paper and answer the question, "Did you graduate from high school?" with a "No." That feeling remained a thorn in my side for most of my life, and it was the reason I pushed my children to do well in school, and obtain a higher education. I wanted them to take advantage of their opportunity, and to be proud of their achievements in their later life—and they are. When we arrived in Anif, we received ration cards for the first time, it was puzzlement to us since the war ended two years ago.

It is now spring 1947.

Ration cards were given to each person in different colors based on age. Each cut-off had a different value for a given item of food. It was new for us to find nothing to buy even though we now had money. The war had depleted all the resources. During the war in Tirol, we had food from Mother Nature, from the farm, and from the little garden my mom made in the meadow. She also knew which mushrooms to eat, and which berries to pick, which gave us a great supplement to what we already had. We were not hungry then.

In Anif, my mother went to nearby farmers to trade for food some items she had made like a shawl and mittens she knitted from the wool of an old sweater Mom also made shopping bags out of corn husks to trade for potatoes and other vegetables. In 1947/48, even though the war was over, we were hungry and could find nothing to buy for the household. I guess we were sheltered in Tirol from knowing the kind of life most Austrians were living, since the *Anschluss* (annexation) to the Third Reich. It was a rude awakening for us.

We thought it would be only a month before we could immigrate to America. But the process was slow, and many of our friends got tired of waiting and went to Canada or South America instead. But my dad held out. He said, "If we cannot go home again, then we will wait to go to America." In the end, it was to take close to five years.

My father and the other men in the barracks raided the woods at night to cut down trees for firewood. He cut a hole in the floor, and made a trap door to hide this wood, because this was not allowed. So did the other men too. Count Johannes von Rohn de Cais, who owned all the land, was told by his forester what the men were doing to his forest. He came to the camp with his for-

ester to ask the men not to cut down healthy trees. He understood
the need for firewood, and promised to mark the trees we could
take, so we no longer had to steal them. This was a relief, as now
the men could go to the forest in the day time, and did not have
to steal wood in the dark of night.

Little by little the small barracks became empty, and the larger
barracks had an available room for us. There were many Czechoslovakian Germans, who were already living in there. We now
got a large room, which was divided into a kitchen and a bedroom. Anna and I had a bed in the kitchen, where it was warm.
Mom and Dad slept in the cold room, with a bed into which they
put hot bricks to heat it up before going to sleep.

I made friends with the Czechoslovakian girls, and I was glad
to have some friends again. Two of these girls were a little older
then I, and one a little younger. Magda Kurtz was older and an
only child, born to older parents. She always dressed like a lady
with a hat and white gloves. We all went to church together each
Sunday. She liked classical music and theatre. Her parents were
over protective of her; she was not allowed to sit in the grass
with us and play. Magda did a lot of acting on her own. Her dad
was able to get tickets to dress rehearsals of the famous *Salzburger Festspiel*, which had resumed after the war. She invited
me to go with her, and I loved it. I remember one Fest Spiel we
saw, *Jederman* (everyman). It was also the time, when I met my
friend, Lisl, who married a soldier after I left. She lives in Texas,
and we are still friends 70 years later. Her mother was the kindest
lady in Lager Anif. She taught me how to sew on a Singer sewing machine with foot pedals. Liesl's family had five children
and she was the oldest. She has a brother that is my brother's
age, and they grew up together. Both were born in Austria.

My brother, Alfred Franz Bachert (Freddy), was born in 1948. He was four years old when he came to America. Liesl's brother showed us around when we visited Austria later. He lived on Alpenstrasse, not far from the camp. I saw the Countess' mansion I worked in, and also the area where the barracks once stood. My son took a picture of the wooden platform the men had made for us girls to kneel on while doing laundry all those many years ago. It is the only visible sign of that dreadful place that gave us a relatively happy communal life. Lisl's grandparents lived there too, along with several other families from their hometown, for which her father was able to find work for at Hoffmann and Maculan. All the men worked for that firm for a long time.

Lisl's Mom let us borrow their metal bathtub she used for her children. It was big enough for Anna and me to sit in and wash well. It was the rule that the children bathe first, then the mom, and last, the dad. Water was precious; we had to carry it in and out of the barracks with a pail from the river by the street. We only had a small tin bowl to use for sponge-baths otherwise. During winter, the men emptied the outhouse, and put the waste on the ground in front of the barracks to make compost for use in the garden. They said the deep freeze would be good to kill the germs, and make the land fertile to grow good vegetables. Every family could plant a garden the size of their frontage. We had two windows, so ours was a good size. It was great, because now we had vegetable soup every day from our garden, along with the half-rotten onions and potatoes we found on the garbage dump across the road in the woods. We no longer were hungry, so the ration cards became obsolete for us.

Just around this time, many American officer's families came to live with them, while they were stationed in Austria. Every Wednesday, the trash from the soldier's mess was dumped in the woods across the street from us. Mom and I waited for the trucks to arrive; we found some unopened cans of pork and beans, along with fresher vegetables and fruit. We were disappointed, because we expected pork in the can, but only found beans, which of course were also welcome. One time we found a mystery fruit. We showed it to everyone, but no one knew what it was. It tasted a lot like lemon, but was not a lemon. We ate it with sugar, and there was not much left after everyone tasted it. We learned later that it was a grapefruit. We had never seen one before. My dad even had grew a few stalks of tobacco in our garden, and of course Mom had flowers. She had something called *Maria Augen* similarly to a zinnia, but with slimmer stalks and fern-like leaves. She planted them to thank the Blessed Mother for hearing her prayers in giving us the chance to plant food again. She also said it attracted pollinators that were helpful to grow a good crop of vegetables. The tobacco leaves were placed underneath the sack of the bed for Anna and me, which had straw in it for a mattress. It was a good place to dry it out. We often checked to see if it was brown yet, so my father could slice it thin and roll cigarettes, which he loved to smoke.

At that time, Mom found out we were getting a baby brother. Dad was on cloud nine, but Mom cried a lot. She knew that babies were a gift from God, but wondered what He might be thinking to bless her at this very difficult time, so late in her life.

The future looked so bleak and scary for us. We were considered Gypsies and called that name many times. We were not welcome everywhere in Austria. It was hard for the Austrian people as well, since they were overrun with refugees during the war. Now, it was 1948. When would things get back to normal? Anif was a small, rural town with only farming families. In Tirol, there had been a different atmosphere; people were welcoming and friendly to us. My Mom had no need to go begging for food there. When she went begging for food from the farmers outside Anif, she often heard, "Gypsy go home!" It was a difficult time for everyone.

On her deathbed, my mother apologized to me, because she took the milk rationed for me to give to my baby brother. She was troubled by that all her life. I did not like milk then, and do not like it now. So, it never bothered me that Freddy got the milk. It was natural a baby should get the little milk the ration cards allowed us. Only by the grace of God was Freddy a healthy baby thriving under such poor conditions, as were we all, since I never saw a doctor or dentist the whole time we lived in. Freddy was born in the hospital in Salzburg, and his birth certificate reads, "Stateless." We were classified as such, and so were any children to our families during this time. When he came home from the hospital, he always threw up after he nursed, so my mother took him back to the hospital to check this out. The doctors had to do exploratory surgery and found his stomach had no opening into his intestine, so he could not eliminate his food. Major surgery for a brand-new baby in 1948! Only by the grace of God did he survive this operation.

At that time, my sister went to Brussels, Belgium, with a group of other children. Maybe it was with UNICEF. To get them healthy, they took undernourished young children to other countries, which had food and willing families to take them in for a few months. Anna left a skinny little girl with pigtails. We missed her, but knew she was well taken care of by a family there. When we picked her up at the train station a few months later, we hardly recognized her. She was beautifully dressed, a little chubby, she had a bob haircut with bangs and curls. She looked like a little princess. Princess Anna we called her. I admired her for having the courage to leave home. She was a courageous child at a young age. It helped her to overcome the bullying in later years in America at Julia Richmond High School, New York, where her accent was laughed at. She showed them all—she graduated with honors! Certainly, something to be proud of. She was the first in our family to go to high school. She had nobody to help her with her schoolwork, as we all did not know anything, especially the new language we were just learning. Her homework was to listen to the radio and repeat what she heard. She paid close attention to key words and was able to translate them. She learned the language of her new homeland quickly and accurately. She was *fresh off the boat* as the saying goes.

Catholic Charities brought clothes for us to Anif. We each were allowed to pick one item per person. Mom never picked anything for herself, she always looked for the biggest-sized dress, with as much material as possible that she could use to make skirts or jumpers for Anna and me. She even knew how to alter little dresses to make jumpsuits for Freddy. She simply crocheted the bottom closed in the middle, just leaving enough room to stick his little legs through. I picked out a mint green jump suit that I loved. It fitted me so well I wore it all the time. It was unheard of at that time in Austria for a girl to wear pants, but the rebel in me never cared what others thought. I made my own rules. I liked to ride my bike with it on, because skirts were a problem riding a bike.

I had an Austrian girlfriend whom I met in a church group and went to dances with on Sunday afternoons, when certain churches had teen dances. Her family owned a greenhouse, and at Christmas they were very busy, so she asked me if I could help by making wreathes and other things. I was happy for the opportunity to have a little job. When I got there her mother asked me to scrub the floor of their bedroom, as she had more experience in making wreaths. I scrubbed the raw wood on my knees with a brush all day long. It was hard work because the floor was very dirty, and she wanted it white, like new. By the time I was done, I was too tired to go home, and it was dark and far away. So, I stayed overnight, as the wreath-makers worked all night. The next day I helped cut the pine branches to the size, which were needed for making wreathes and other items for the cemetery at Christmas.

It is an Austrian custom to take care of the family grave at the town's church cemetery, the same way you would care for a flower bed in your own yard. They plant seasonal flowers all year, and cover the grave with a blanket made from pine branches during the winter. It looks quite nice when you visit a church cemetery in a small Austrian village, even if you know nobody there. Anif's cemetery has a celebrity buried there. It happened after I left, but I heard the family had the graveside service at night for privacy. It is the famous and legendary symphony conductor, Herbert von Karajan. He was born in Salzburg in 1908. He is Salzburg's second most famous son, after Mozart. In 1955, he was appointed music director for life of the Berlin Philharmonic. At my friend's family nursery that fateful evening, I brought food and drink from the house for the workers. I ate with them, and had a good time. We had no way of communicating with my parents, but I thought it was okay for me to stay overnight, as they knew with whom I went, and they would not be worried. But my mom sent Rolf, the oldest boy from the family across the hall in our barracks, to check on me. We hung out together often with all the other *Lager Kinder* (kids from camp). He was the oldest of us. He left me there as I was okay, and went home to tell my mom. The next day, I had a fight with the girl who was my friend. She told me I looked like a clown in that mint green jump suit on my bike. I told her off in no uncertain terms saying, "You are jealous. It is only because you are too dumb to know that American girls wear these types of outfits. And furthermore, you are too fat and ugly to fit into something like this!" I got on my bike and left, and we never spoke to each other again. I got no money for my work, but I did get dinner. If I only I could tell the American girl that donated that jump suit to her church, how much I appreciated her gift, which was sent overseas to give to refugees like me, "Thank you little girl, whoever you are. Your good deed brightened my life for a long time."

We also got a C.A.R.E. package once, after Freddy was born. We shared it among some families in the barracks. There, too, was a mystery item which no one knew. It was peanut butter, we found out later. We also found out it was good to eat. Spam was the most loved by all. There was a donor's address in the package. So, I sent a letter thanking them and explaining my family situation to them. I hope they got it, and were assured that it was most appreciated and the money was well spent. Mom made potato soup and put a little spam into it, which made it a thousand times better. I can still taste the goodness of that meal.

I also remember a blue knitted little dress Mom found in the pile of donated clothes. Since there was nothing for a boy toddler, she took that little dress with an idea of how she could make it suitable for a boy. She had wool in a similar color blue, and crocheted a closure at the bottom of the skirt leaving enough room for two little legs to come through on either side. She made it into a boy's jumper. It was beautiful! It was the only thing she could fix for Freddy. It was so clever, it was the talk of the camp. It looked so good on him and admired by all. His blond hair and blue eyes brightened up, when he got his new jump suit. He was the cutest little boy in the world. Later on, when I worked for

the Americans and he was
older, I took him to Mira-
bell Park in Salzburg on
Sunday afternoons, and
the soldiers we met there
who knew me, thought he
was my child. They said,
"He looks too much like
you to be your brother."

Anna, Käthe, Alfred Franz Bachert,
Welcoming our baby brother, Anif, Austria, 1948

Freddy was born on Janu-
ary 28, 1948, a day before my father's birthday, which was another precious thing my father enjoyed all his life. Anna and I
were allowed to pick names for him, when he was born. I picked
Maximilian and Anna picked Alfred. So, his name became Alfred
Franz. My father's name was Franz. My brother Freddy now has
a son born in Florida, who also carries my father's name. In retrospect, when I look back at my family's endurance, both during
the war and after, I consider myself blessed to have such a normal, healthy family. Thanks to my parents, who worked so hard
at this new beginning in their middle age in America. They were
able to enjoy their golden years in peace and harmony among
us, enjoying our children, as well as seeing their own children's
accomplishments. I thank God that my father said, "If we cannot
go back home, we are holding out for America." The promise of
getting us into the American Sector of Austria was so important
for us that it made it very welcoming to Dad. Americans did not
give visas to people they could not investigate.

Waiting, Winter, & Washdays in Austria

One day, the mailman brought me a notice to come to the post
office for a phone call. I wondered who could be calling me.

My curiosity was piqued, and I started out to Anif in the snowy, icy weather the next day. Anif had nothing to offer except the butcher shop, a bakery, and a milk farm where we got our infrequent food rations. My father earned union wages, but there was nothing to buy in town. The only additions to Anif we appreciated back then were the church, the post office, the cemetery, and the railroad station.

My mother used to go on the train at 5:00 am to a better butcher in Salzburg that occasionally had horsemeat for sale. It cost half of the ration card, so it was a good deal. She always brought us smoked sausages, which were delicious. We could all eat one, little frankfurter-type sausage that day. In my mind, I can still taste their goodness.

I preferred to go to the bus station for the trip to Salzburg. It was the shortest, direct route on the autobahn. To take the train, one had to go up the hill, around, and through the town to the railroad station. On the trek to the Anif post office, I was so very cold, as my clothes were wet and frozen by the time I arrived. I gave the postmaster my note, and she directed me into a closed wooden phone booth in the corner, where I was to wait till she made the connection to my caller. It was warm and delightful in that booth, and I did not mind waiting at all. The connection took so long that the snow and ice had melted from my clothes and my shoes, and made a puddle on the floor beneath me. I could not get up and leave to use the toilet, even if there was one, for fear I'd miss my call, but I could not stop the urine from leaving my body too. To my dismay the puddle under my feet grew so much bigger now. I thought that the trip home would be even worse, since even more of my wet clothes would be frozen on to my body. I was in a very stressful situation. I was embarrassed at what happened, and angry at whomever called me for putting me into this situation.

I never had seen a telephone before. That was a treat! I waited and waited, and finally, the phone call came through. I said, "Hallo," and it was a boy from Lager Haiming, who missed me so much he went to all this trouble just for the two of us to talk. I was not happy to hear from him, of all people, as I sat in that puddle in the phone booth. I was furious with him! I called him names and hung up. I picked up my sloppy self, left the phone booth and went straight to my home in the barracks. There was with no way of cleaning me up before the ice melted from my body. I explained nothing to my mother, and did not want to talk to anybody for a time. I often think of the boy, and wish I could apologize for my rude behavior. But I did learn from this a lesson for life. When I supervised the PS 63 school yard, I often told the girls in when they complained about a boy liking them, "It is an honor if a boy likes you, but you do not have to like him back. Just smile and walk away." It saved many a school yard fight. And I thought of Otto from Lager Haiming Tirol. I hoped he fared well in life as I did. The next day, the postman came looking for my mother, and told her about the miserable thing her daughter did in the post office. Well, it was not just an embarrassment for her, but also for me. What if my friends found out about this? I was more embarrassed than before. The post office personnel knew it was not just melted snow in that phone booth. My friends never mentioned it to me, so if they knew, they kept it to themselves, and for that I was deeply grateful.

Washday in Anif was a tricky situation. We had no large basin to wash clothes in, so each item had to be washed separately in the tiny metal bowl. Mom heated the water and washed our clothes as well as she could. After the first round in this bowl,

we continued washing them in the stream, that ran next to Alpenstrasse. The stream was near the road where there was a bridge
to cross into the development. Next to that bridge, we were able
to get down to the water easier, as the ground was elevated, and
we rinsed the soap out of our clothes in the stream. We had to
be careful not to let them slip away, as it was hard to get down
on the side of the bank to retrieve the clothes, before they were
carried away by the current. I remember the cold, cold water
numbed your hands, so you could not feel your fingers and
could not hold the clothes. The strong current often claimed gar-
ments you could not afford to lose. When that happened, we ran
down the bank, and were able to retrieve our few and precious
clothes with a stick. To make the job easier, the men soon made
us a wooden platform next to the bridge to create a more even
ground to work from. The water was still ice cold, but now we
could kneel on the wood, and have a little more control of the
clothes we had to rinse. Luckily, we did not have much to wear,
so there wasn't a lot to wash and rinse. We wore the same clothes
all week, except on Sunday, when we put on Sunday dress for
church. On Monday, the week began with washing, but the clean
clothes were likely to be the same as we wore the previous week.
My mother always said, "It is not a sin to be poor, but it is a sin
to be dirty." Most of the families had a broom handmade by our
fathers. We swept our room every day, and took our shoes off
when we entered the room.

Salzburg was near where grandfather had stayed, but we could
not cross the border that divided Austria to get him. Based on
the stories we heard, and what my grandfather later confirmed,
it was good we had run away from the approaching Russians. At
that time, Salzburg was just emerging from the smoking rubble
left by the heavy bombing during the war. They were glad to get

refugees to help with rebuilding the city. Salzburg's old town, where Mozart was born, stayed mostly intact.

I loved the old town of Salzburg. Getreide Gasse and the cathedral were not bombed. I admire that the US airmen's surgical-like bombing saved these landmarks. My father's main job in Salzburg was building Café Winkler on the Mönchsberg overlooking the old city. When Tom and I visited Salzburg in 2008, we went up Mönchsberg. Walking around, we found what once was Café Winkler is now a finer, more sophisticated place. Only the clock tower was left, as a reminder. The view is still the same. Overlooking Old Town Salzburg is a treat. I remember the abbey on Mönchsberg, and also the cathedral where I so enjoyed going for Sunday high mass. I also saw that Salzburg and Hellbrunn have grown so close together now. No train station; not even train tracks were left. At the time I lived there, I walked at least a half hour in snow and sleet on the autobahn to get the bus to Salzburg. I loved going to the city when I had time to spend there.

It just so happened that late in the summer of 1947, Grav Johannes's mother, who lived in a mansion in Hellbrunn, needed help getting washed, dressed, and assistance with other activities. Her mansion was full of refugee princesses, and whole families of royals from Hungary and Poland, because Hitler had persecuted them as well. Some worked for the American underground [Secret Service?], and had to leave home in a hurry. One such man was a Hungarian prince, who left his wife and young child at home, while he lived in exile in Austria, continuing his work with the Americans. Two Polish princesses also worked for the Americans in Salzburg, and took the train to work from Hellbrunn every day. Princess Katiana was older and took care of her aunt's household. Since money was running low for them too, they could not afford servants any longer.

One day, Princess Katiana came to our barracks to ask for a young girl to be her aunt's companion. She had not much money to pay, but she could promise a nice room, good food, and pleasant work for a young girl. Some of my friends did not want to live away from family. But for me it was an opportunity to get away from our sad circumstances, and to live in a real house with heat, hot water, a bathtub and flush toilet, and even a bed for myself, which I had never had before.

With a new baby coming, I knew my mother would be happy to have the extra space. I remember how attentive she was with the baby of the family in the small barracks, where we lived before. She had no time for Anna and me then. I imagined how preoccupied she would be with our own new baby. It was time for me to grow up, and be brave enough to leave home with the Princess Katiana to help the Countess von Rohn de Cais in Hellbrunn.

Just as we were leaving the house for my new job, a car came by containing three men from the Russian zone. The car stopped; they were looking for my mother. All the tenants of the barracks went out to see what was happening. We never had a private car stop at Alpenstrasse 8. It turned out to be two doctors, who smuggled my grandfather, Johann Brucker, out of the Russian Zone of Niederösterreich to bring him to us in Anif, using another person's papers. He had become blind, and had no one to live with. There was no communication other than the mail service in those days. My grandfather had a letter from us with a return address on it, and that is how these people, out of the goodness of their hearts, took the chance to unite him with his daughter.

It became even more important now that I leave this place, I thought. My Opa needs my bed. He had been treated well by the Russians. He could speak Serbian, and was welcomed by the

Russian soldiers, and he cooked for them. They gave him plenty of food to eat and vodka to drink, which was all he wanted. These doctors helped our grandfather out of the car, said good bye, and quickly left. By the grace of God he was well and they were not caught. The chances these men took to do this was amazing. Russian soldiers were not kind-hearted during WWII. Thank you doctors for doing that kindness for a stranger in need. You will be rewarded in heaven. As Opa Brucker was living with us now, he got the bed in the kitchen. Anna made a bed in the room my parents had to themselves for a while. Freddy's crib was next to the window to the right of their bed, and Anna's bed was put in the corner to the left of their bed. Thankfully, I was gone and on my own, working in the mansion in Hellbrunn. When I came home to visit, Opa always asked me to get him hard cider, which he loved to drink so much. But I always said, "Opa, it is very far to Anif, and I have to go back to my job in Hellbrunn very soon." I am sorry I did not do this little favor for him, as he had nothing else in life to look forward to. Even to get to the outhouse was a chore for him, as he had nowhere to hold on the whole length of the long hallway in the barracks. Every family had a crate next to their door to store their things. I am sure he ran into many of them. It is a wonder that he found our door on his way back. It was so dark in that hallway, that even I ran into crates to and from the barracks entrance. At this time, life was better for the family, as Mom had her garden, and ration cards were not needed much anymore. The citizens of Anif were friendly to the longtime residents of the barracks. As they got to know us, they saw we were law-abiding citizens, working at whatever jobs were available. We were invited to plant seedlings of fir trees several times in the woods for the Count to restore his forest, I remember.

I also remember the two daughters of the farmer, who we got our milk from when we had ration cards. They were not so friendly at first, but later they were okay with us girls from the camp when we joined the Anif church youth group. We developed a nice camaraderie with them.. When the American Army officers were able to bring their family to Austria, many of my DP friends got household jobs with these families. The Austrians had no jobs for us and were not able hire DPs anyway. It was the law to hire only Austrians, except for construction jobs and to clear the wreckage of the bombed-out buildings. They scraped off the cement from the bricks to re-use for new construction. Some of the boys I knew had such jobs. Schools became operational again, but after age 14, DP children were not allowed to attend.

ℭ

Chapter Eleven

Hellbrunn:
Countess von Rohn de Cais (1947-49)

My room faced the rose garden. I had a comfortable bed next to the window, which was open most of the time. I enjoyed hearing the birds sing and looking at the stars at night.

I was in love with Loden coats! They were made of a particular green/grey color with fancy buttons made from the horns of bucks. They used the same material to make the national dress Austrians wore like a uniform to show their proud heritage. If you've seen the movie, *The Sound of Music*, you might remember the captain, who wore one of those lovely Loden coats. I thought, "When I have money, I will get one just like it." The money I was paid for being the companion to the Countess of Rohn de Cais was enough to pay a seamstress to make me one. It had to be custom made for you. Nothing like it could be bought in the Anif stores, as all of Austria was depleted of material goods, due to the war. Even school books, paper and pencils were nowhere to be found.

I did not attend school and tried to work. The perfume factory turned us down for work also. So, the option was to live in the mansion in Hellbrunn where I would have a whole room to myself—not just a bed—was inviting. In retrospect, it was a good move for me. I learned to like poetry. The Countess liked me to read them, and other stories to her. Reading and learning became a lifelong joy that never left me, and one that I shared eagerly with my own children. When my daughter, Debbie, was little, I worked at the school, and ran the mimeograph and xerograph machines to duplicate the work for the classroom teachers. I always made one extra copy for her to play school with me at home. That was a plus for her, because Bobby, my son, had to rely on my sparse knowledge from my limited schooling to learn from. But I get ahead of myself.

My job with the Countess was wonderful. I loved her like the grandmother, that I left behind when we left our home in Indjija, and she loved me like her own. I did find my grandmother many years later living in Stuttgart Lager Zuffenhausen, Germany. The Countess always just called me *Kind* (child), never by my name. I kept busy getting her dressed for the day, or undressing her for the evening. We walked in the formal gardens, which had clearly seen better days, and we sat on a bench in the rose garden while I read her poetry or books. She enjoyed it tremendously and it all was fun for me too. It gave me some of the education I missed in school. My love of poetry followed me all my life. I have written many poems, mostly about nature that God created. I am in awe often at the natural beauty of Western North Carolina, where I now live. It is a little like Austria with many open spaces, green meadows with wild flowers, and grazing cattle and horses. The mountains are not as high as in Austria, but pretty green also.

All over Austria life had changed, even for the rich and famous. The Countess von Rohn de Cais' mansion was across the railroad tracks at the far end of town, and there were almost no houses around it. The grounds were so overgrown with shrubbery that you could not see the house from the street. It was set into a large garden with overgrown rose bushes, behind an ornate iron fence with a high, heavy iron gate. It became a haven for other royalty, who were persecuted by Hitler's forces when their country was taken over.

The whole lower level was rented to an extended family, with older and younger people who did not mingle with anyone. They spoke a language I did not understand. On the second floor, was only one public room remaining; all the others were occupied, rented to fleeing royals from other countries. The Countess's bedroom was located in a corner suite next to the two rooms, where her nieces from Poland slept. The other corner suite was the residence of a Hungarian family of four, including the elder Count von und zu Linderhof, his young wife and two daughters. One daughter was a little older then I, one a little younger. They did not mingle with others, as they only spoke in Hungarian to one another.

The Countess had a son, Graf Johannes von Rohn de Cais, who lived in Anif in a castle surrounded by a moat and a park. He lived there by himself with only his servants. The Countess's two nieces from Poland were Princess Katiana and Princess Maruska. The sisters were in their late twenties. Princess Katiana later became her aunt's manager and Maitre d' Hôtel. Princess Maruska worked for the American military in Salzburg, most likely continuing the work she had started in the Polish underground army. The corner suite occupied by the family from Hungary were both *from* and *to*. In other words, they were high up the aristocratic ladder. Count von und zu Linderhof was an interesting gentleman; a very personable man, he always wanted to talk to me. It helped that he spoke very good German. His wife the Countess von and zu Linderhof was much younger, but was also very friendly to me. The two teenage daughters did not mingle with me. They let me know that I was not up at their level socially. Or, perhaps they simply could not speak German, as only Hungarian was spoken within the family. The Countess came into the kitchen to make dinner for her family often while we, Frau Greenblatt and I were there. Her German was good and she made us feel at ease. She wanted to know all about my homeland and asked if I knew what happened to the royal family there. I was not acquainted with any aristocrats, nor did I know of any living in my hometown of Indjija. Mrs. Greenblat was a local Austrian woman, who had known our Countess a long time.

Next to the kitchen was a bathroom suite the size of a large in America. It was a closed room with a flush toilet with a wooden seat, the size of a large table top. The seat had a hole in the middle on which you sat reading a magazine while going to the bathroom. Next to the bathroom was another room with a large, glass, double door, where a six-foot-long bathtub sat near a double sink, a medical scale, and towel racks. It was used by almost everybody for bathing in the house, except by my Countess. She had a wooden arm chair with a lid for a potty in her bedroom to use privately. I cleaned it out every morning when I got her dressed for the day. She had a sink, and large carafe for water that I kept filled. I had to be sure that she had everything she needed in her room at all times. The only job I did not like was cleaning her potty every day. She was a nice old lady, like my grandmother, so I got used to doing that chore.

Next to the staircase was my room, and next to that lived the Hungarian Count von Pappenheim. He worked for the Hungarian underground. He continued working with the Allied Forces in the hope he could help liberate Hungary from Communism, which of course he did not achieve. We all know that the 1945 Treaty of Yalta with Stalin was not kept, and it gave the Allied forces grief for a long time. But Communism was now openly alive and well in Hungary, as it was in Yugoslavia. Count von Pappenheim left Hungary in such a hurry, that he only had a small picture of his wife and his young son, and no other belongings. He showed this picture to me with an aching heart; he clearly missed his family very much. His German was only passable, but we understood each other enough to get by. He was hardly ever home, except to sleep. Both he and Princess Maruska worked for the Americans in Salzburg. They took the train to Salzburg from Hellbrunn each morning. They also ate in town before coming home.

At that time, England advertised for maids in the local newspaper. Austria had many refugees, who only were allowed to work as maids or construction workers. Princess Sofia von and zu Linderhof signed up to go to England to be a maid. When she left, I remember the family crying. At the time, I did not know the details. Later, her mother obtained a British newspaper article with the princess' picture in it under the headline, "Hungarian Princess Works as Maid." I did not read English, but her mother told me what it said.

My room faced the rose garden. I had a comfortable bed next to the window, which was open most of the time. I enjoyed hearing

Salzburg

the birds sing, and looking at the stars at night. It was the nicest place I had ever lived. I loved my house in Indjija, but we had no indoor plumbing, and the outhouse was a far walk. It was cold in the winter to walk to it. Since we left home, I had lived in army barracks with no comforts of home at all. In my new job, I was happy and felt like a princess, with a real room and a real bed. I liked having the bathroom most of all. It was comfortable to go to the bathroom and so close by; it was practically ten feet away from my bedroom. I had a desk, a closet, a chest of drawers, and a refrigerator in my room. All of this was not needed, as I had nothing to put into them.

I liked to write letters on my desk. Gretl in Salzburg was my best and closest friend, and we wrote to each other often. There were no telephones in houses back then. One summer, during the *Salzburger Festspiele* that started up again after the war, we hosted an actress friend of the Polish princesses at the mansion. She was performing in a play nearby. She probably shared a room with the princesses, as there were no spare rooms. This was circa 1948/1949.

I also loved taking long baths in the large tub at night. It was my favorite thing to do while listening to music. I must have been overly long one night, since someone in the toilet room, stepped onto the wooden seat to look through the window into the bathtub suite where I was bathing. I was shocked to see eyes looking at me! First, I hid in the water, then when it was all clear, I got out quickly and went to my room. I have always guessed that it was the old Count von and zu Linderhof, even though he walked with a cane. I suspected him to be a prankster, who had nothing to do and nowhere to go, with too much spare time on his hands.

One night, one of the princesses came to my room to ask if I knew what happened to the Blessed Mother statue, from the shrine she had in her room. It had disappeared. No room was ever locked, but I never went into any room other than my Countess's bedroom, and the living room which also became her dining room. Her Blessed Mother statue was often misplaced, and it was a mystery. Frau Greenblatt was gone for the day, so she had no one else to ask. She knew I had not seen it, but was desperate to find it. I could only lament with her as I was catholic too, and knew the value of respect for such a statue. I don't think Frau Greenblatt would take away someone's statue of the Blessed Mother. Once again, I suspected that the old count had played a trick on Princess Maruska. I never said that to anyone. I only felt sorry for the princess. The next day the statue appeared as if nothing had happened.

The Princess Katiana cooked fairly well as a novice to that job. She fired the cook, and became the Maitre d' Hôtel for her aunt, as she needed the money. She cooked a Mediterranean menu of mostly local vegetables and some meat, all brought to the house by local farmers. She used a cookbook, and the meals were always ready at noon. I would bring the Countess in from our walk in the garden, and would help her get ready for dinner. Dinner was at noon, and still is in Austria. Countess Katiana served for the two of them in the dining room. Frau Greenblatt and I ate in the kitchen. My countess often napped for a long while, so I had

nothing to do but talk to Frau Greenblatt, while she cleaned up
the kitchen. She knew I liked to go to dances, and she encouraged me to go to a neighboring town on a certain Sunday afternoon to meet her niece. We went to hunt for a dress to wear in
one of the steamer trunks in the attic. The attic was full of bats
that hung from the rafters. When we opened the door and turned
on the light these bats were startled, and flew away through the
little porthole windows in the attic roof. We came away empty-
handed, as everything was high style junk from long, long ago.
Soon after, Frau Greenblatt brought me a dress, which she had
gotten from a friend's daughter about my age (I was 16 at the
time). It was a beautiful cornflower blue dress with a pleated
skirt, long sleeves, and a white collar. I loved it! It was the nicest
dress I had ever worn. It fit me perfectly, except it was a little
short. Frau Greenblatt let out the hem as much as possible, so the
dress almost reached my knees.

I felt like a princess, as I rode my bicycle to that town to meet
Frau Greenblatt's niece. We met and talked, and little by little
more of her friends joined us; some girls and some boys who all
were nice—I thought. When the music started to play, they all
paired up and danced without me, never to be seen again. After
a while, I went home puzzled. Where did they go? What had
just happened, I could not even guess. When Frau Greenblatt
arrived for work on Monday, she could not wait for my report.
I could tell she was happy for me. I told her my story, and she
could not believe what happened either. The next day she told
me that her niece's friends were embarrassed by my short dress.
Well, so much for trying to blend in with Austrians again! I was
left to wonder, was it the dress? Or was it the fact that I was a
foreigner? As a DP, we did not have to wear an arm band, as the
Jews did during Hitler's time, but it was a stigma just the same.

I will never know, and now I don't care anymore, but it did hurt for a long while.

I wrote to my friend Gretl and told her what happened to me and how fed up I was with the Austrian teens. She was Austrian too, but she was kind and inclusive. I don't know what town she was from. She was a maid in the home of a US Army captain and loved it. She suggested to me to get that kind of job too. Americans are very nice and generous. I got a fraction of the pay that she received, but she did all the house work for them. I only spent time with my Countess and did some personal care for her. I had fun and could not call it work at all. When I got my job, the Countess Katiana told me the pay would be very little, as her aunt was running out of funds. Money was not necessary to me, as there was nothing to buy anyway. I just wanted to have a room and a bed all to myself and indoor plumbing instead of carrying pails of water in and out of the barracks every day. Life in the mansion was like a fairytale for me then. I would have books to read and poetry to learn; that's all that was important in my world then.

To be a companion to a countess sounded magical, and it was. It was one of the highlights of my life to meet and learn from these people, who helped me grow into a caring, well-rounded person. The generosity of my Countess moved my heart; to take in all these people who had to flee their homeland. The royals, who previously had servants to do everything for them, were now cooking and caring for others. Even Princess Sophia von und zu Linderhof became a maid in a land where she knew nobody, and where her title did not matter. She had no famous father to fall back on. The Polish Princess Maruska working with the Americans before and after the war. The Hungarian Count von Pappenheim, who left in the middle of the night without his family.

He worked with the Americans to keep his homeland from falling under communist rule. They all became willing to do what
they needed to, in order to survive, and to make life better for
others. I only hope Count von Pappenheim was able to get his
family out of Hungary, as surely, he could never go back home;
just like I could not go home again. I have great admiration for
these people, and am forever grateful having met them.

It soon got to be fall and winter. Frau Greenblatt had help cleaning the one public room and my Countess's bedroom. These
rooms had ceramic tiled stoves, almost as high as the ceiling,
which were heated with coke, all winter. I had to carry buckets of
coke upstairs from the basement to keep the house warm. Once
a year in the spring, Frau Greenblatt hung the Persian rugs on
the clothes line in the yard and we beat them, while Frau Greenblatt's helper cleaned the parquet floors.

My mother and I had a big conflict that first spring, because she
wanted to keep my salary for when I got married. Well, there
was no way I was going to give her the money to save up, because I feared it would get spent. If she needed money, I would
give her some, but I never relinquished my right to manage my
own affairs. She did not need money, as my father got paid good,
union wages, and there was still nothing to buy after the war.
Every store was depleted, and mostly shut. This conflict was re-
solved quickly. My mother agreed to let me keep my money.
She agreed the days of the old ideas were gone, we lived a new
culture now. I was in charge of my own destiny. She well remembered what happened to her money at age 12, when she was
a maid in Indjija. At the end of her year, she wanted her money,
but it had all been given to her father during the year, and there
was nothing left for her. She agreed with me, and we remained

friends forever. Her aim was always
to help her children, never to hinder
their growth.

I was sixteen years old now and
wanting to have a little free time.
The only free time I had was after
church each Sunday. The Countess
and I took the train from Hellbrunn
to Anif to church each week. Afterwards, her son took her to his castle
in Anif for the afternoon, and I went
home to see my family. I went up-

Maria, Franz, Käthe, Alfred Franz
Bachert, Hellbrunn, Austria
Sunday outing in the park, 1949

stairs to worship from the choir where my friends sang, and then
we went home together at the end of mass. Often, we left after
Holy Communion as we thought mass should be over by then
anyway. We inhaled the incense, watched the candles flicker on
the alter, and felt an inner peace. We often walked around the
formal gardens in Hellbrunn to watch the goldfish in the ponds.
Sometimes we just ran and played catch on the way home.

It was nice to see my family. Freddy was cute, Anna liked to read
the funnies in the newspaper, and my Opa Brucker asked me to
fetch him some cider, which he often liked to drink. I always had
to tell him it that was too far for me to go to get it in the short
time I had off. I usually got back to the mansion in Hellbrunn
around 5:00 pm. More and more frequently, I arrived and saw
the Countess on the balcony pacing, looking for me. As soon as
I came through the iron gates I heard her voice, *"Kind wo warst
Du so Lange?"* ("Child, where were you so long?") I told her it
was only five o'clock and I was on time. But that did not matter
to her, she wanted me by her side all the time.

Castle of Graf Johannes von Rohn de Cais, Anif

Sometimes, I had to meet her at her son's castle when she slept there. That castle still stands at the foot of town of Anif. It sits behind a moat with a bridge—a real medieval castle. I hated to stay there. It was dark in every room, and the eyes in the portraits on the wall seemed to follow you wherever you went. The only good thing was I liked talking to the kitchen maid. She was a young girl like me, and a stateless person also. I don't remember what country she was born in, but she was not Yugoslavian.

CR

Chapter Twelve

Salzburg and Captain Brody's Home (1949-1951)

He told me once, "Kitty, you can fry chicken like a Texan."
The more he praised me, the more effort I made
to please the family.

My friend, Gretl, kept telling me to take a job with the American officers. One day, her lady employer asked her if she had a friend looking for work. A friend of hers was coming to live in Salzburg with her husband, who was a US captain, and she was looking for a girl to be her maid. Even though I could not speak English, this friend would be interested in meeting me. Gretl was an Austrian, but not from Salzburg. She liked working for Americans as she had a Lithuanian boyfriend whom she loved, who was waiting to immigrate to Canada. Gretl also wanted to go and was applying for entry into the United States, as well. America was much too long a wait for him. He had no family to consider, so he went to Canada. She, too, went to Canada. Her boyfriend wanted a new start altogether, so Gretl met some other Lithuanian man in Canada, whom she married.

I met her lady's friend in Salzburg, who was temporarily living in a hotel, awaiting a housing assignment. The lady said I could come every Sunday to spend time with her three-year-old daughter, Kathleen, at the hotel. I agreed. I enjoyed my visits with this little girl, and we went to Mirabel Gardens, the puppet theatre, and other interesting places around the hotel. When that family got their housing assignment, they asked me to be their maid. Well, I was 16 years old, and did not know how to be a maid, but that was okay with them. Apparently, their daughter chose me from all the other applicants. They liked me, trusted me, and it felt good to be chosen. Mrs. Brody said not to worry about anything, and that she would teach me how to be a maid. And also, she would teach me the English language, as she saw the book I had acquired to learn from and said, "That is not English that is British. We don't speak that way." Gretl was delighted, since I would be in Salzburg near her and she and I could resume an active friendship.

I gave notice to the Countess and soon went to the home of Captain Brody and his family. And so, I left the castle in Hellbrunn and started a new life.

Little Kathleen was three years old, and most days, she and I were left alone all day. Mrs. Brody was a teacher for the Officer's children in Salzburg. Kathleen liked to sing children's songs and rhymes, which I learned from her. She also prayed a special prayer at night, "Now I lay me down to sleep, I pray the Lord my soul to keep. If I should die before I wake, I pray the Lord my soul to take." This prayer stayed with me always, and I taught it to my children and grandchildren.

I learned a lot from this little girl, as we did many fun things in the afternoon when my housework was done. She especially liked going to the amusement park nearby. I liked going there too, because there were some nice young boys working there, who flirted with me. I loved my job. I especially liked cooking the captain's favorite dinners. He liked fried chicken and coconut layer cake the best. He told me once, "Kitty, you can fry chicken like a Texan." The more he praised me, the more effort I made to please the family. I studied their American cookbook, using my German-English dictionary, and made notes about how to cook their favorite food. I liked them and they liked me—it was a win-win situation.

The only thing I did not like was ironing the captain's uniforms. After I washed them—in a machine, not the cold, cold brook that we washed our clothes in in Anif—I put them in the freezer rolled up tight to keep them moist. Then, I ironed them the next day it went much smoother and faster. I wanted to get that job over with quickly. The captain often used two uniforms a day, especially when they went out to special events at night.

I loved reading bedtime stories to Kathleen, because I had never heard these fairytales before, and I enjoyed them tremendously. Some nights, the captain would read to his daughter, but mostly, I had the treat of doing so myself. One day, I punished Kathleen for something she had done by not reading to her. I can't remember what she did, only that it must have been a small thing I am sure. She was a sweet little girl and nearly always followed my direction. Well, on that evening, I had a date with one of the boys from the amusement park, so I wanted to get my chores done quickly. It all backfired when the captain asked me to read her a story that night, as he had paperwork to do. He made Kathleen promise me that she would never commit this small crime again, so I had to read to her. Sadly, I missed my date, but that was okay because that boy no longer was employed in the amusement park, as he did something bad. I was not told what it was.

Now, already over 17 years old, I had thoughts of working in the Post Exchange (PX) as a waitress, because I would have more time off, plus the soldiers came through the PX. The army post was within walking distance of my old Anif barracks. But I could not go there to live, as my grandfather had the bed in the kitchen where I once stayed. But I was ready for a change and dreamed about what to do next. The day after my story reading to Kathleen had made me late for my date at the park, she and I visited the carousel, as we did most afternoons. I looked around, but my date from last night was not working. I asked around, but nobody knew when, or if, he was supposed to work again. Kathleen and I had our fun, and we went home skipping and singing as always. After supper and her bedtime story, I want up to the third floor to my room. The maid who worked for a lieutenant and his wife, who lived on the second floor, had a room near mine. She told me her lady received a package of clothing from home in America that she wanted to share with us. I was to come upstairs the next afternoon to meet her. Her lady was very friendly, young, and beautiful. I loved her at first sight. She had a bunch of things in her living room for us to choose from. Her maid, Frau Elisabeth, was a grandmother from Yugoslavia. She had a young family living in Hotel Europa, which was a residence in mid-town Salzburg for displaced persons. We both admired the lovely things the young lieutenant's wife offered us—we had first pick before she took it to a local church for distribution. I chose a sweater and red wedge sandals, and a dress. I also got a white pair of rubber galoshes, all of which I loved. I thanked her profusely and took my leave, smiling from ear to ear. Kathleen and I were headed back downstairs, when the lady opened the door for us and said to me, "You are welcome." I was confused. Why would she say, "You are welcome," to me now? I knew the word meant *willkommen*, which means to welcome a person in to the house, but I was going out. Well, I was too happy to let that exchange spoil my day, but I was totally confused. I learned the English meaning of this phrase much later. In German we say, "*Danke*" (Thank you) and answer, "*Bitte*" (Please).

After work that night in my room, I dressed up in the lovely things I got that day. More and more, I learned to identify with the Americans, who were the nicest people I had met since leaving my homeland. I thought of my shopping trips to the PX with Kathleen and her mother. That too, was a nice experience for me. My mom and I could never go, because we did not have military privileges. My shopping trips were much less exciting. Sometimes with my mother, or sometimes alone, I would make trips with a ration card and stand in a long line. We always hoped the store had food to sell us, as meager as it was. I walked a mile to town to the farm to buy milk and to the bakery, where we got bread, standing in line forever. Those were not pleasant shopping trips. They were shopping trips out of necessity, and a chore not a pleasure.

I remember when the captain's wife bought me my first Coca Cola fountain drink. On Saturdays, we often shopped and lunched at the PX. It was a Sunday meal for me to have a hamburger and a Coke. I had never tasted anything like it before, and it was so good. My mom made hamburger patties for us, mostly filled with stale bread to make enough for the family. So, I dreamt that working in the PX would give me access to a burger and a coke every day. I saw other young girls like me, working as waitresses there—most of them DPs like me. In 1950, after

Herta, Elsie, Kitty (me)
Waitresses showing off, US Army Post
Hellbrunn, Austria, 1951

over a year at the captain's, my English was very good. So, I gave notice to the captain's family, and applied for a job at the army camp in Hellbrunn. I got the job as a waitress in the PX, and I was thrilled.

I was employed at the PX from 1950 to 1952, so now I was really on my own. My new job as waitress in the PX was wonderful. I learned very quickly what I was to do. Sometimes I worked behind the counter, other times on the floor as waitress. As the counter person, my responsibilities were more than just waiting on the boys. I had to fill the syrup into the coke machine and juice machines. I had to keep track of all necessary supplies, so we never ran out of needed items. I was happy doing either job.

The US Army also gave housing to all their employees, and a car service to and from the job site. It was in another part of Salzburg I did not know. I also did not care where it was, as I stayed on the base as long as possible. I was always there when they needed someone to work. I had a room to myself in yet another abandoned German Army barracks, in another part of Salzburg. I was amazed at how many camps there were in Austria. I had lived in three by then. The US officers lived in mansions the German Army officers had lived in before. No wonder most Austrians I had met were not happy with the Anschluss. This camp was large like the ones in Tirol. It was outside of town, not on my familiar side of town. I don't really remember the neighborhood, as I spent as much as possible time at my job. I was happy there with all the young, happy, smiling soldiers, and the friendly welcoming girls I worked with. There was music in the PX, very loud music all the time from the jukebox. I loved it! I knew all the American country music stars like Patsy Klein, Hank Williams, and more. As it was winter, it was no fun to get around on foot in Salzburg. So, I loved the white galoshes with my red wedge sandals inside them, and wore them every day that winter.

It was not long before I had a boyfriend. He was my age, as were most soldiers who came through the PX. The Korean War had started by now, and the boys had to go on maneuvers in the woods. I volunteered to go by van with some others from the PX, to bring some favorite snacks to the boys. My picture ended up on the cover of *Stars and Stripes* magazine. The boys were fun; friendly and talkative. Later, I met a few in New York, in the Social Security office, after they returned from active service. I was there getting cards for my family and myself. I was the only one who spoke English in my family, and would fill out the forms for my mom, dad, sister and brother. At night after work, the chauffeur took me back to my apartment. Several other girls worked on base and lived in the barracks with me. It was fun when our boyfriends came to visit, and they could see that we were one happy family. I especially remember one girlfriend, who was a refugee from Hungary; her name was Herta. We were like sisters. I even went to the Catholic church services on base on Sundays. I made the base my home away from home, and I was happy there. I asked one of the soldiers, who was Catholic, to get me a missal to read at mass in English. He did give me one, and I still have it to this day. I thought that when I got to America, I should know how to pray in English.

CharChapterter ThirteenThirteen

Bremerhaven, Germany: Waiting for America (1951-1952)

*Catholic Charities took us by train to Bremerhaven to wait
in yet another former German Army camp;
thankfully, it would be our last one.*

In 1951, right around summer, my parents sent for my uncle, Mom's step-brother, Franz Brucker. He was to come and take care of his father, because we were going to America. Opa Brucker could not go to America, because he was blind and had also lived in Russian sector of Austria. We had not applied for a visa for him. So, my mother thought her step-family should take their father to Pernegg, Steiermark, in Austria, where they all lived and worked. My Opa, Johann Brucker, knew he could not go to America with us. He told my mother the same thing he told her in Oberösterreich, when the Red Army approached. He said then and now, "You go and take care of your children. You must do what is best for them. I am an old man; my life is over, so do not worry about me. I will be fine wherever I am."

My grandfather and his son Franz had lived together before, when they went to work in Germany together. Franz moved in with his mother and sister, when he came back from that job. At this important time, my mother contacted him for help with her father. He and Lissi, his sister, both worked in a furniture factory that provided housing for them in an old German Army barracks (where else?!) in Pernegg near Graz, Austria.

Franz returned my mother's message saying that his mother refused to take her husband back after all these years, and as he and his sister lived with her, he could not help out. Franz came to see me at the army camp, as my parents did not have a mailing address for me. I actually did not know the address where I lived, because the chauffeur took me to and from work. I thought, when I talked to my Onkel Franz, he could live with Opa and Lissi with their mom. He did not like that idea at all. It was a sad situation, because any day soon, we would be ready to leave for America, and we would have to do so without our Opa. We loved him, and wanted a good home for him in his old age.

My Uncle Franz explained the situation to me, but under the circumstances, I still thought he should do something for my Opa, who was his father. He said his father needed care and they (Franz and Lissi) worked all day, and their mom had no intentions of caring for him. They could not move and leave their mother alone, as she would have nowhere to live. The housing was provided by the *Moebel Fabrick*, (furniture factory), the firm they worked for. In the end, Opa had to live with strangers in an old people's home when we left. My parents bought him Austrian citizenship, so he could be admitted to a nursing home, which my parents inspected before taking him there. We were sad to see him go there, but we could not take care of him any longer, since we had already been interviewed and accepted as permanent residents in the US. It was only a matter of time before we would be able to leave for good. We knew he would be taken care of physically, if not mentally. So, we left him with a heavy heart, but it was our future that my parents were thinking of, so it had to be this way no matter how sad it was.

I am still amazed at how many forced-labor camps the Nazis had in Austria. The grandeur of the mountains was spoiled by the valleys with all these barracks littered across the meadows in lower Austria. Now, many years later, I can see the beauty of this land, which was marred by these scars. So, now in Bremerhaven I see them in Germany also. The port of Bremen was surely used by the Germans, as it is now by the Americans.

When my parents applied for our visas to immigrate to the United States, they had our birth certificates translated into German from their original Cyrillic Serbian, which we could not read. The Hotel Europa in Salzburg became a refugee residence after the war. Thankfully, some countrymen of ours were staying there, who could vouch for us. It was important to have this done quickly, the paperwork had to be accurate. Then, we were waiting to be interviewed by the American authorities. It took a long time for them to do background checks on us, but soon we were called in. Our interviews went very well. The US Army officers who conducted the interviews were friendly and nice. We were asked to swear to uphold the Constitution of the United States, and also to bear arms (even me) to defend our new country, if the need arose. Of course, we all said yes. We had no homeland to defend, and if we did get a homeland, it most certainly would be defended.

The idea of defending one's homeland was old hat to my father, as he was once an Austrian citizen. His own father, Adam Bachert, lost a leg in WWI, and then died from his wounds, fighting for the Austrian Empire. My Dad, the oldest child in that family, was only 14 years old at that time. Austria lost the war and had to give back a third of the Austrian Empire, which included the land of Indjija where we lived. It then became the Kingdom of Yugoslavia. The assassination of Arch Duke Ferdinand was the trigger for that war. At that time Dad got a new citizenship without lifting a finger. He became a Serbian National. So then, as a young married man, he was drafted to do military service for a short time in Split, on the Adriatic coast (which is now in Croatia). He left Indjija along with the other men and saw the beauty of this part of his homeland, which he did not know before.

After the Archduke Ferdinand was assassinated in Sarajevo by a Bosnian Serb in 1914, the Serbians were not sure of the loyalty of the German-speaking population. That man was against the marriage of Serbian Princess Sophie von Chotkova to the Austrian Archduke. It was a political marriage, he thought just to gain more land for the Austrian Empire, and the Habsburg Dynasty.

King Alexander eventually became ruler of The Kingdom of Yugoslavia, which became our new homeland until WWII. In 1944, we were forced to leave by Marshal Tito, who was groomed by the Russians to govern Yugoslavia after WWII. He never let German-speaking former residents back to his country, and we became stateless people.

Back to our hopes and dreams of becoming Americans.

In February 1952, the day finally came when our ship came in, it would be our last former German Army camp to live in. A large

USS General M.B. Stewart,
Refugee ship sailing to America, 1952

room full of strangers occupied the many bunk beds. Open stall showers for hundreds were lined up in separate buildings. It reminded me too much of the Lager Kufstein where we were sent to live after the war in 1945. The big difference was that, the place there was locked and patrolled at night, and this place was open. We were free to explore this region of Germany, which was on the North Sea. The weather was mostly foggy, and a drizzling, cold rain fell often. We must have been in this camp for weeks. One ship came and went, but we were not allowed on it. We waited, and waited, for the next one. As it turns out, it was fun waiting in this camp with many other future permanent residents of the United States. We were there for a few weeks until that wonderful US Army ship, The USS General M. B. Stewart sailed in. We had witnessed people leaving before, but now it was our turn, and we were very happy to go.

In the meantime, we enjoyed ourselves the best we could. We shared a room with a nice family with four boys, from Semlin, a nearby town back home, where my step-grandmother lived. We became close friends. They left a week before us, and went to College Point, New York. We remained lifelong friends with that family. I was especially thankful to their mother, Mrs. Klein, because she had the same shoe size as I did, and in a gracious gesture, she shared her shoes with me often.

In that holding camp, the young people got together for some social affairs, dances, and the like. I was still traveling with my white rubber galoshes, and my treasured red wedge slippers, which were not good for dancing. Mrs. Klein gave me her shoes for those occasions, so I could go dancing. There was a single young man in our room as well, who went strolling along the waterfront with me, and we loved to dance together. He had a camera, and liked to take photos of me all around Bremerhaven. I never did get any of those pictures, it was not possible to develop a film there. He met me in New York when my ship arrived, but I did not want to continue our friendship. I wanted a brand-new start in my new homeland of America. He complained about that to Mrs. Klein and she told him, "Forget about her, she only liked you because you have a camera." I was a little hurt at the time, but in retrospect Mrs. Klein was right. My friend Richard and I parted as friends saying, "Das ist schicksal." It is fate.

☞

Chapter Fourteen

Crossing the Ocean in 10 Days

One night, we all got up before dawn, as we heard land was in sight. ... In the dusk and fog, it looked like a string of pearls was strung in suspension from heaven.

Our 10-day ocean voyage was uneventful. The minute we stepped on board the USS General M.B. Stewart, we had a fire drill and were told, "You are now the property of the US Army." We had to strictly follow all directions from the officers. In Salzburg, during our interviews, we were asked if we would carry arms to defend our new country, and of course we all said yes as we truly wanted to be upstanding citizens and belong to this land, that took us in and gave us a home. We all wanted a second chance to have a normal life of our own choosing. All we could think was how wonderful that would be. I did not think that our first moment on the ship was the time to start exercising that

newfound freedom of belonging to the US Army, I found out
what they really meant later.

We were assigned jobs on the ship, because there were only a
few crew members on board. The primary purpose of this ship
was to transport soldiers to Germany, and to return to America
for a new batch of troops to send overseas. So, in return for this
free ride, everyone had to pitch in to do a job. Four of us young
women, who could speak English, were assigned to the Officer's
Mess to work in the dining room. We were sent to the officer's
quarters on an upper deck. We were given a schedule to follow;
each of us had duty serving the food to the officers. We were assigned a room for four, with two bunk beds. I don't remember
which bunk I had. I only know I was comfortable the whole trip,
except for a few weather conditions, that nobody could predict.

I have a memory of some days, such as when I set the table
for breakfast and the dishes rolled to the other end and onto the
floor. I was not aware there was a storm, but the ship rolled so
badly, that one could hardly stand up and walk outside on deck.
That was the only time I was a little seasick, and the symptoms
went away fast. The other ladies were older but nice to me, we
had nothing in common except we all spoke English. It was fine
with me. I enjoyed seeing all those stars at night, and the crisp air
with sprinkles of the sea splashing on my face. The white foam
and the choppiness of the water was a wonder to me.

It was a wonderful experience. I loved it. I only thought of what
it would be like to live in America. What the people would be
like. What kind of job I could get, and who my friends would
be etc. I did not see my family at all, but knew they were okay.
Dad was in the men's bay, with all the other men who all had
jobs to do. My father worked in the laundry, where it was hot

and smelly. He had a bad time all day in the laundry. Unfortunately, he told us later, he was seasick from the minute the ship set sail, until it berthed in New York. He looked skinny when we saw him in New York. Mom, Anna, and Freddy were with the other woman and children in a separate bay, so I did not know if they were ever sick, or not. Other than missing my family, it was fun running after the cups on the dining room floor. The officers were nice, but not talkative like the boys in the army camp in Hellbrunn. They had an important job to do with little help.

One night, we all got up before dawn, as we heard land was in sight. We watched and waited to see. Finally, a glimmer in the distance! We strained to see it. In the dusk and fog, it looked like a string of pearls was strung in suspension from heaven. As we got closer, we saw Manhattan Island dressed in lights, shining through the fog all along the East River into the bay. I was in awe at that sight. So were most of the others. I think my heart was racing.

Suddenly, Lady Liberty rose into view, and waved to us. Well, you can imagine, there was not a dry eye on that ship. Everyone was filled with gratitude and overcome with emotions. No one uttered a word, anticipating what was to come. We were all too stunned and in tears to speak. All of a sudden, a patriotic song started in a low voice by an anonymous person. To this day, I hear that quiet voice whenever I hear the American national anthem played anywhere. It still stirs up emotions, which make me cry each and every time I hear it.

Even now, I remember that pearl necklace around Manhattan, as a welcoming sign for us. We arrived in New York on an early Saturday morning, February 22, 1952, at 8th Avenue Pier and 42nd Street. I felt I was finally *home* as soon as I stepped on to

Family Bachert, Arriving in America,
8th Ave., NYC, 1952

the asphalt of Manhattan, I was *home*, and New York City became *my* town. I was a new person. I thought now, "I finally have a home!"

It was a very moving day at the pier that morning with people coming and going and the crate my father made in Indjija for this trip was standing there holding our scant possessions.

A lot of people were at the pier looking to hire workers of all kinds. The Catholic Charity volunteers said we were free to go wherever we wanted to, as our sponsors in Iowa no longer needed us. Our sponsors were business owners in Dubuque, Iowa. I have a copy of the ship's manifest with our names on it. I think they sponsored us through the Catholic Charity Organization, which helped refugees after WWII. We were offered to be sent to any state we wished to go to. We had to agree that after we got settled, we would pay them back. Dad said, "I did not come to America to make debt, I want to work right now. I have no wish to go anywhere else. New York is fine for us." Some people said they heard California was a good place to live, so they went there.

Katie Buschbacker & son Bobby (L),
Oma Juliana Flehr Bachert, Anne & Fred
Bachert, NYC 1956

We kept in touch with our countrymen for a while, and they did do well in California, the state they chose to call home. We always loved New York, and I still do. The lady from Catholic Charities took us to another part of the terminal, where people looking for workers spoke to us through translators. I knew English, but my family did not. They needed all kind of workers. This is how we met Mrs. O'Connell from Far Rockaway. She needed someone to build a wall around the open showers on the porches of the bungalows she rented out for the summer. The wall was a new requirement by the city, which came into effect that summer, and she had to comply before the renting season began in May 1952.

Renting her forty bungalows was her livelihood. She was a widow with two teenage sons. So, my parents signed up for this job and the Catholic Charity lady said we could always contact her, if this job did not work out. But the determination of my parents made it work out. As they often said, *"Aller Anfang ist schwer."* That is, "Every beginning is hard," as they had both learned in their young lives in Yugoslavia. When they got married in 1927, and went to France for a year, not knowing the language, to save a nest egg for building a house for their future family.

I wrote my Opa right away, and he shared our happiness. My parents got a report that he was doing well, and was well taken care of. A year or so later, we were notified that he fell down a flight of stairs, and died. I think that my Opa, a proud man all his life, probably fell down those stairs on purpose, because he had nothing and no one to live for anymore. Several years later, my mom received his black Iron Cross from his gravesite in Austria, which she kept in her house in Astoria, NY. She brought it with her to her retirement home in Florida, where it stayed till my father's death in June 1997. Then, she had a marble slab made for this cross to match my father's grave stone. She put this cross on top of my father's grave, in front of his stone, to combine the two in St. Joseph's Church Cemetery in Jacksonville, Florida. So now my Opa Brucker is with his family in America after all.

While still in Austria, my American serviceman boyfriend, at age 19 or 20 years old, re-enlisted in the US Army. His name was George Hofflink from Covington, Kentucky. He gave me a ring—where he got it from, I don't know—it was antique-looking with a purple stone. I loved it, and wore it every day even after moving to America. We considered ourselves to be engaged. We were both naïve as to what engagement really meant. At 19, I was his first girlfriend, and he was my very first boyfriend. When I moved to America, I wrote him from Far Rockaway, that we should go our separate ways. He wrote me that he also thought breaking it off was a good idea. Our paths would never cross again. Well, that ended it a little sadly, but it was welcomed by us both. I sent him the ring back, and wished him well.

Soon after, US soldiers from Austria were sent to Korea to fight in the war there. George had already re-enlisted, and the last I heard he went to Korea in 1952/53. My parents and I soon moved to New York City, and George and I never heard from each other again. I hope he returned from Korea safely, and had a happy life like I did. It seems ironic that my husband of 49 years, Lorenz Buschbacher, served in the Marine Corps during the Korean War as well. He was not shipped to Korea, because he was only a permanent resident and not a US Citizen, at that time. His tour of duty was serving in the crash crew at Cherry Point North Carolina's naval airbase. Might George and Larry have met in Korea?

Crossing the Atlantic Ocean in 10 Days

By Katharina Bachert, age 19

A lonely ship taking us to destinations unknown

Chopping up the waves through a silvery foam

A host of stars light up the night, like a soft

Blanket protecting the Heavens out of sight

I am humbled by these majestic views full of wonderment

I gaze into the Firmament, is this a beginning or an end?

A shooting star catches my eye, reassuring my thoughts

Going by, yes, bad days have come to an end

Dawn will soon be breaking, we are all anticipating

At the end of this journey will be the rainbow's end

A vision in our heart, reborn, ready for a new start

The azure sky now overhead will bring our ship to Heaven-sent

℞

Chapter Fifteen

Far Rockaway (Spring-summer 1952)

The pool house had several old bathing suits for people to use when they came from Manhattan and did not bring one. I tried them all and liked them all. I just liked American clothes!

Even as we learned English, the German language newspaper was a household possession. We learned about this paper in Far Rockaway, where we got information on jobs etc. Much later, in Astoria, Queens, my parents ordered a newspaper from Germany called *Donau Schwaben*. It connected us to some of our former neighbors living all over the world.

Mrs. O'Connell's home was a Victorian mansion at 9 Norton Street, in the Bayswater section of Far Rockaway. It was in a row of well-groomed large homes, along the bay. Dr. Grossinger's home was on the corner before this blue mansion. My parents had a large room in the attic for them and Anna and Freddy.

First, we enjoyed the scenery and a tranquil life in Far Rockaway. My parent's job was restoring bungalows on the ocean for
Mrs. O'Connell. After a hard day's work wallpapering rooms,
then cleaning up the cement from my father's work of enclos-
ing the outdoor showers on the deck, they came home and my
mother had to cook for her family. She was given chicken feet,
discarded by the butcher, and vegetables by Mrs. O'Connell for
soup.

I did not live there. Mrs. O'Connell got a job for me with her
neighbor, a doctor in Manhattan, who already had housekeepers
from Austria, Herr Hans and Frau Maria. I was the nanny for Dr.
Grossinger's two little girls.

My parents and siblings were happy to have a job and a room in
the attic of this beautiful house on Norton Street. It lay between
the bay and the ocean in a quiet neighborhood, not yet bustling
with people who only come from the city to enjoy the beach all
summer and party. Freddy went with Mrs. O'Connell all around
town, riding in her Cadillac, but only if he could ask in English.
He quickly learned by saying, "Please can I go with you *mit.*"
(*Mit* means with.)

Mrs. O'Connell was a lifelong friend to us. She visited my parents often when she came to Manhattan. At one point, she arranged for a friend of hers to take me to the telephone company to interview for a job. Soon enough, I took the train from
Far Rockaway to lower Manhattan, which was a long train ride.
The train started out on an elevated track through Queens, then
wound up underground in lower Manhattan. This was a marvel
in itself for me. The lady interviewing me was hostile. She asked
me where I lived, and when I told her, "Norton Street, Far Rockaway," she snapped at me and said, "That is *Northern* Street." But

I did live on Norton Street, not Northern Street, but was afraid to say so. I was shocked at her tone and frightened of her, so when she told me I was not ready for a job at NY Telephone Company I was glad. I was also glad that my parent's work was done in Far Rockaway in June 1952, when all 40 bungalows were up to code and renting season began. My mother loved those little houses, and hoped to have one for her family one day. After all the work they did there, they looked like new again. Mrs. O'Connell told her if one was left over after the rent season was over, they could move into it. But that never happened.

Austria was bitter cold in February when we left there, but in Far Rockaway it was warm and sunny now. I traveled across the continent in white rubber boots, a pair of red wedge-heeled slippers, and a long sweater over a long-sleeved dress from the lieutenant's wife, which I loved. But now it was warm, these clothes were not good to wear in this weather. I also had leather ski boots, hand-crafted at the same time. Austrians wear ski boots all winter, even if they do not ski, because the snow and ice on the road never melts till late spring. Frau Maria wanted my outfit so badly, that she offered me two dresses for it which she had got from Mrs. Grossinger. She said she would never wear them, but Mrs. Grossinger wanted her to have them. I liked the American clothes she got from Mrs. Grossinger, who was an actress, as they were stylish. Something, Frau Maria never would wear, as she was the typical Austrian *Hausfrau*. Her husband was there also, but he wore just regular pants and shirts much like all other working men. So, we traded two dresses for my Loden skirt suit.

On my first day off work, I put on a black, strapless dress with a Bolero-type jacket, and went to Far Rockaway to window shop. I looked at everything—even me—in the store windows. I liked the way I looked. I came to a card store with picture postcards from Rockaway Beach. They were beautiful, but to whom could I send a card? I thought of the friends I left behind, but only my friend, Gretl, would be worthy of a card like this. Gretl was waiting for a visa to Canada, to be with the boy she loved. And she might have left by then.

I kept on window shopping, when a nice looking, young police officer stopped to talk to me. He asked all about me, then he asked where I got my dress. I told him, and he said I looked nice, but that it was not the kind of dress to be worn in the daytime. It was meant to be worn at night for going to a party. I did not know there was a different kind of dress for day and night. It seemed strange to me. I thought, once you are dressed, it is for the whole day. Still, he was interested in knowing all about me, and I liked talking to him. I missed grown up conversation, since I was with the Doctor Grossinger's two little girls all day and late into the evening sometimes. Those little girls depended on me while their parents were at functions in Manhattan many nights. Frau Maria and Mr. Hans could hardly speak English, and they were glad we could speak our Austrian dialect with each other.

So, this nice police officer asked if I wanted to meet him that evening when he got off work. I said yes, I was free till the next morning. He said he felt obliged to tell me that, in America, if a police officer asks you for a date and you do not want to go, it is okay to say no. He explained that a police officer was just like any other person in that respect. So, I thought about it and said, "No, I will not come back tonight. I will visit my parents instead." He smiled at me and said that was okay. We shook hands and parted. I thought of that as being a nice polite way to be friendly. But I knew my time in Far Rockaway was limited, and I did not want to start a friendship at this time.

When I got to my parent's house later that evening, in the driveway were the two O'Connell boys and a friend, who was a mechanic in a garage with a small black car. I admired it and told them so. The three boys often tinkered on cars in the driveway. Ronald, the friend with the black car, asked me if I wanted a ride in his car. I said "Yes." The only time I was in a car was when Mrs. O'Connell brought us to Far Rockaway, from the boat dock in Manhattan. In Austria nobody had a car, we all walked everywhere, or took public transportation if it was available, and that too was uncertain.

After that night, Ronald and I became good friends. We spent many evenings riding in his car to the beach. We walked in the sand, held hands, and flirted. I had a nice time with him in Far Rockaway. It was an innocent teen friendship. I loved riding in his car, and he was glad to share the experience with me. He was so proud of that possession. He polished that little black car every day. I never saw him after we moved to Manhattan in the summer of 1952.

I also had the job of answering the telephone in the Dr. Grossinger household, as Frau Maria's English was not as good as mine. I took a message for Mrs. Grossinger by writing the telephone number as I heard it, "Circle 6 - 1000." I made a circle and wrote down the numbers. This was most confusing to Mrs. Grossinger. She told me that in America, we write the two letters of the name of the exchange, followed by the number. CI for Circle 6- would be CI6 - 1000. I told her that in Austria, nobody has a telephone in the home, not even the American officers. She was surprised by that. I told her how we had to go to the post office to receive and make phone calls. I told her of that dreadful day I had to walk in the winter's blizzard to the Anif post office. I never forgot that.

Dr. Grossinger's home had a swimming pool. I loved going in the pool, even though I could not swim. I was lucky that the two little girls were smart, and listened to me about staying out of the deep water. The pool house had several old bathing suits for people to use, when they came from the city (Manhattan) and did not bring one. I tried them on and liked them all. I wore a different one each day. I just liked American clothes! That had all started with a mint green jumpsuit in Anif from the American Catholic Church donations.

Dr. Grossinger never trusted me to do the right thing for his children, and yet it was strange that he had hired me to be with them for so many hours while he was away. In the house once, he bolted into the bathroom when I was there with one of the children, to see what I was doing. I had never encountered such a suspicious person before, and it was so odd. Much later, I heard from Mrs. O'Connell that he was arrested for selling illegal drugs through his office in Manhattan.

CR

Chapter Sixteen

Moving to Manhattan
(Summer 1952)

With old newspapers, we polished the glass entrance door until there wasn't a spot on it. Mom swept the street in front of the house every day, so that part was easier on Saturdays.

After about three months in Far Rockaway, we moved to Manhattan where Dad became the building superintendent of 331 East 83rd Street. The apartment was a dungeon, but with no money and no other job, my parents were delighted to find it.

We moved to Manhattan on advice from our countrymen and friends from home, who arrived in New York a week before us in March 1952. To us, they were seasoned veterans on how to make a living in our new homeland. If you became a building superintendent in an apartment house in Manhattan, you got free rent, a

Katie Bachert, Front steps of
83rd St. apt, Manhattan, 1952

small salary, as well as time to look for a second job. And that is exactly what Dad did.

All the houses attached to each other along 83rd Street, and were six stories high. This style of building is called brownstones. The main house had fairly nice apartments, but the superintendent apartment was a dungeon. It's no wonder that the city condemned these apartments just a few years later. You entered our basement apartment from the street, underneath the concrete steps leading to the front door of the house upstairs. There was an iron platform, which led to the stairs down into our dark space. The only light that came in, was from a window under the staircase looking at the gray cement of the street, and located in back of the house, through which coal was delivered for the furnace. As you walked from front to back, you encountered an enclosed flush toilet on the right wall, and a dumbwaiter next to it, through which my father pulled down the garbage every night from the apartments upstairs. He prepared it for city pick up every Wednesday and Friday. My mother separated the salable items, soda cans, and bottles. She also kept the newspapers, and bundled them for sale to the Boy Scouts once a month. These newspapers were a teaching tool for us all. My mother read the pictured ads and learned the words for food items. She kept a careful look out for which grocery store had a sale on items that we needed. My sister Anna liked to look at the comics every day, my little brother Freddy cut out pretty animal and car pictures to play with. We also used the old newspapers to clean windows and the glass entrance doors of the lobby in the building upstairs.

Across from that area was a small kitchen with a table and some rickety chairs. My parents did their best to make it a home; they white washed the place several times to get the coal dust off. The single, hanging lightbulb shed just enough light to see the constant march of cockroaches. Dad put up a shelf for the one or two pots we had, and we actually loved having a bathtub and sink

Katie & Maria Bachert, Kitchen of 83rd St. apt, Manhattan, 1952

in the kitchen for our baths. Next to the kitchen was a small space that became my parent's room. It held their bed with just enough room for Freddy to have a small bed next to it.

The next opening was our living room. There was one, large window, which gave us the view of the cement enclosure at street level, that surrounded the iron platform and stairs to enter the basement. In the living room was a new sofa bed my parents had bought with the money they got from Mrs. O Connell. This bed was for Anna and me to sleep on at night and also for sitting on during the day.

Dozens of pipes, that delivered utility services to the tenants, crowded the ceiling above our heads. They were covered in years of dust and spider webs, which were almost impossible to get rid of. The place was pungent with coal dust that smelled foul, and was unhealthy to breathe, but none of us suffered any lasting ill effects from it. In the winter, it was impossible to be comfortable, because the heat created by the pipes delivering steam upstairs were hot all the time, and there was no way to let the heat out. Nevertheless, my parents, Anna, and Freddy lived there for many years, until they saved enough money to buy a house in the Astoria neighborhood of Queens. I left when Larry and I got married in 1954.

All of us, except Freddy, worked to pay for living expenses. Dad worked as a bricklayer's mate, because he didn't pass the test required by the union to hold full bricklayer status. It was not steady work. He needed a steadier income, so he got a job as a grinder at a tool and die manufacturer for airplane parts. Dad also had to do minor repairs in the apartments, such as fixing water leaks for tenants, and whatever else that needed doing. Mom cleaned offices at night, in the business section of the city. I worked for Pepperell Manufacturing Company, as a file clerk, and Anna went to school. Freddy, at age four, stayed home with Mom, as she had to be home all day to receive packages for tenants of our building. Anna and I were responsible for the care of the lobby of the apartment house. That was the only time Anna and I had a conflict, as I wanted to get up and do the job to get over with quickly, while Anna liked to read the daily comics in the leftover newspapers first.

Every Saturday, Anna and I polished the brass mailboxes and doorknobs in the lobby of the apartment house. We also mopped the six-story staircase, and cleaned the bannister with furniture polish, as it was made of very nice wood. We polished the glass entrance door with old newspapers, until there wasn't a spot on it. Mom swept the street in front of the house every day, so that part was easier on Saturdays. We finished this job in a few hours, so I could do my personal laundry by hand in our sink in the kitchen.

Mom was good at finding opportunities to earn money. She be-friended some of our tenants, who knew of Austrian families on

Lexington and Fifth Avenue, who liked to have Viennese dinners cooked for them and their guests. My mom was able to do this, and Anna and I could help. She made strudel at home to take with her, when she did these dinners on weekends. They loved her authentic, home cooking. I helped her to serve the more elaborate Viennese dinners she cooked for them on weekends.

Mom struggled a bit with the language. I remember once when Mom had an argument in a store. She yelled at the clerk, "You think that because I can't speak good English, I am stupid. I can add, and know how much this pocketbook costs. I saw the sign in the window last week and saved the right amount to buy this pocketbook for my daughter for Christmas." Of course, the proprietor came to rescue the clerk, and apologized to my mother. Anna had expressed a liking for this pocketbook during one of our window-shopping trips, and Mom wanted to surprise her for Christmas with this special gift. This was a common immigrant experience to be misunderstood.

Exploring our new Manhattan neighborhood was fun. From Lexington Avenue east to the East River was only a few blocks to walk. It was a nice, quiet, middle-class neighborhood of mostly mom-and-pop stores, and six-story row houses. On the East River, on York Avenue was Gracie Mansion, where the mayor lived. A Catholic church was there too. All that was important to us, was within walking distance. Third Avenue was mostly residential, and so was Lexington Ave with high-rise apartment buildings.

Central Park was close by. It was a great place to go exploring. A very important thing for us on 86th Street. was the subway entrance. It was considered Yorkville, named after General York. Many Germans settled there in the 1920s, opened Ger-

Family Bachert's first trip to Central Park, 1952

man restaurants and specialty stores on 86th Street. Schaller und Weber was the butcher shop for wurst, and Café Geiger was full of Austrian Pastries. In Café Geiger, one wall was full of showcases with torte and strudel, and the other side was lined with bistro tables for coffee and dessert. On Sunday afternoons, they had classical music concerts. It was a favorite place of mine.

On 86th Street, there was also the five and dime store called Woolworth, another favorite place for me. Every payday, I stopped in for something to buy. I bought dishes and drinking glasses to replace the jelly glasses that Mom initially used. I also found very nice earrings and make up at Woolworth. All of this was a luxury to me which I never had known. It was all new and I was excited by all the possibilities.

Also on 86th St., the store windows had televisions playing for all to see as they walked by. It was the first time we ever saw a television. We went to see it at a certain time of day, when they had a program of interest. Sid Caesar and Imogene Coca were a famous comedy team back then. Their program was called *Your Show of Shows*. Everyone thought it was so funny, but to me it was stupid. In later life, my children always said, "Mom has no sense of humor." Sometimes they were right, though I have always laughed at different things from nearly everyone else. I liked living in the city. The subway line took me all over this wondrous town. I met two girls close by, and we became friends.

They took me to the movies and dancing in Schwaben Hall. They were German-Americans and liked going to the dances there. That's where the boys were. New immigrants frequented this place, and they played the music that we liked to dance to. It was a great social hall at the time.

At that time, I was walking down Second Avenue, just around the corner from where we lived, and saw a sign for help needed in the window of a delicatessen store. I went in to ask about the job and was hired on the spot. My English was good enough to have a conversation with the customers, and I could make change from the cash drawer without help from a mechanical cash register which, in this case, was not available. That job lasted only a week or less. I was fine helping people with items from the store, but the trouble came when I had to make a sandwich. When someone asked for a sandwich, "With everything," I did not know *not* to put mustard and mayo and relish on it. When they asked me to slice their pickles, I literally sliced them into little pieces, instead of in half. I was really confused by all this. The American style of eating a sandwich was unfamiliar to me. Then, a man asked me to put his sandwich into aluminum foil. I knew aluminum to be a hard metal. How could I wrap a sandwich in hard metal? I had to go to the kitchen and ask the owner to come out and do this. She showed me what aluminum foil was, which we did not have in Austria. While I could speak English well enough, I was still not used to everyday American life. But I would learn. I said goodbye and thanked them for the kindness they showed me.

In Austria, we eat our wurst dipped into mustard and without bread. As a child in Yugoslavia, smoked ham or any kind of cold meat was eaten with good bread on the side, but never wrapped in bread. We know the English Earl of Sandwich invented the

sandwich, but it never became popular in the rest of Europe. It
goes to show you that not only the language is important in your
new country, but also the customs.

Some of the younger ladies I met took me to restaurants, the
Paramount Theatre to see special shows, to Cony Island Amusement Park in Brooklyn, and the Giants' baseball games. In fact,
they told me, and I believed it till Larry told me otherwise, that
in order to play on that team you must be a giant. They really did
look tall to me. What did I know? I never saw baseball before.
I only knew soccer, because that is what Austrian boys played.
They also told me in order to ride the rollercoaster in Cony Island's Amusement Park, I must sit in the last car. I believed that
also. I guess I bought the Brooklyn Bridge a few times as well. I
loved to learn about my new homeland. I always wanted to blend
in, and not stand out as a newcomer.

It was 1953 and I had a new kind of social life in America, and I
enjoyed it. But getting ready to go out was different for me than
for most of my friends. I first had to do my laundry, then I could
do my hair and nails to get ready to go out with my friends from
Pepperrell in the evening. I never spent money on hair or nail
salons, I saved as much as possible for a brighter future. But I am
getting ahead of myself a little. My job at Pepperrell comes next.

Working at Pepperell

I met my friend, Magda at a dance in Schwaben Hall Magda was
born in New York, but spoke a little German, as her parents were
German. Magda invited me to her house sometimes to watch
TV, but nothing I liked was ever on. Her family was very nice,
and they wanted to know how things were in the *old country*. As

their parents came to America many years ago, they were glad to have escaped the strife.

Magda had an older sister, who worked for a manufacturing firm in Lower Manhattan. Pepperell Manufacturing's sales office was on lower Broadway in the Woolworth building. I went to meet Magda's sister on Monday at nine o'clock in the lobby, and she would take me to the personnel office. I found the building with no problem, and was amazed at how many people came in to work. I waited and waited, but nobody talked to me. So, when it quietened down I got up to go home, disappointed. I did not know what this girl looked like so I thought maybe I missed her.

Just then a young girl in a blue business suit walked up to me, and asked if I was Katie. My heart dropped ten feet as I said yes. She apologized for being late, and we went to the personnel office on the third floor. The secretary gave me some papers to fill out, told me to wait, and said that Mr. Ferrini would talk to me soon. I was delighted to meet him in his private office. It was decorated so nicely, and I thought it would be a great place to work. Mr. Ferrini and I had a long conversation. He asked all about my previous work experience, all of which was not related to what they were doing in this firm. He knew that I was fresh off the boat, and said if I wanted to start as a file clerk, he would hire me. I was on cloud nine and could have kissed his feet, but I politely said, "Yes, Mr. Ferrini."

When I left his office, the secretary gave me papers to take to the filing room for the supervisor there, and told me she would tell her I was coming in. Then she called the general supervisor and introduced us. He was a mild-spoken man in his 50s, who wanted me to call him Mike. That was very strange to me, as in my culture you do not call an older person, especially not a boss, by his first name. Mike took me to Hazel in the filing room, and she showed me what my job would be. I was to file sales slips for the stores that ordered sheets from our salesmen. I would have the file drawers labeled from A to M. That was great, and I understood right way what I was to do. Hazel did not file away papers. Instead, she alphabetized them, and got them ready for me to file in the folders already in the drawers. There was another person also filing papers like me, and she worked the rest of the alphabet. Hazel also had to get papers out for secretaries, who worked on accounts, as well as for the salesmen. The filing room was large with a six-foot wall on three sides, and an opening in the front with a counter for people to ask us for papers when there was a question, etc.

I reported the next day bright and early, eager to work. I actually enjoyed that job for two years until my first child was born. When I got married, the company gave us bedsheets as a wedding present. They were more than I ever saw in my house in Indjija, where we had white sheets to sleep on. But, once I got pregnant and it showed, I was told they could not have pregnant women working in a sales office. It just could not be done! As a courtesy to me and my good work, Mr. Ferrini allowed me to stay an extra month, but after that I had to leave.

In the meantime, I was promoted to assistant PBX telephone operator, out of sight of the sales staff. The two operators, Lucy and Gertrude, needed help as one could not handle the busy switchboard if one of them got sick. Pepperell sent me to the telephone company for training for a week. I was so happy, and hoped to meet that nasty lady, who corrected me with the way to say Norton. I wanted to thumb my nose at her, but never saw her.

Lucy and Gertrude were my most favorite friends in Pepper-ell. Lucy had the warmest Italian family in Brooklyn. No matter when you visited, there always was a feast on the dinner table for you to take part in. Lucy was to be my maid of honor at my wedding. She and I talked about it often. She was happy for me to have such a nice guy as Larry to marry. She hoped to find one just like him. As it turned out, Larry's brother was not in favor of Lucy being my maid of honor. "The family is first," he said. If he decided not to come to our wedding, then none of the Buschbacher family would be there. I did not want to start my marriage in that way, and Larry agreed. His brother suggested instead that Lucy be a flower girl instead of a maid of honor, and that he and his wife were to be best man and maid of honor. Lucy did not want to pay the expense for a dress for bridesmaid, so, sadly, she did not come to our wedding. We drifted apart after that. So, Gertrude and John attended and their daughter, Alice, was the flower girl. My sister, Anna, and Larry's cousin, Eva Buschbacher, were the bridesmaids.

It was a nice wedding party in the end. Gertrude and John were lifelong friends. They had a long marriage, and now have two grown children; one in college and one in high school.

While I was still working at Pepperell as file clerk, I met a retired soldier from my days as waitress in the Hellbrunn army camp. We were shocked to see each other across on the other side of the ocean. We greeted each other like long-lost friends. It seemed he had gotten his old job back, when he returned home from the war in 1952. He was a junior sales representative for Pepperell. We met when he needed some papers for his account from the file room.

One day, there was another young man at the counter to ask for papers for his sales account. We recognized each other from the Hellbrunn army camp. He called me Kitty, as I was called back then. But now I was called Kathy, so I was startled when I heard Kitty, which I did not hear in America. Now I had a more sophisticated version of my name, I thought. What fun it was for us to reminisce about that time we passed together in Austria. I told him of some other retired soldiers who I met at the Social Security Office when I was there with my father to get his card. A few of the boys I knew in Austria arrived home safely at that time. He said that when the Korean War broke out, most of the soldiers had to go there to fight a new war. He was lucky his tour of duty was over and could come home. The army was taken out of Austria soon after I left, and sent to Korea in 1952. He asked if I heard of my old boyfriend, George, who was his friend also. No, I told him as he re-enlisted, and had gone to Korea. I told him I sent him the ring back as soon as I arrived in USA, we did not correspond any more, and I hoped for the best for him and also my Captain Brody. I am sure all the families were sent home then, and that little Kathleen went back to Texas to her friends and extended family. I hope she remembers me fondly, as I remember her. Thank you also to Mrs. Brody for the English lessons, and the fine lunches in the PX on Saturdays. The hamburger and Coca Cola still taste good in my memory. I think of her whenever I eat a fast food hamburger. She was a teacher in school for the officer's children and at home with me. I loved her. She often said she liked having me in her house —me, who knew nothing about being a maid—so she could teach me to do things the way she wanted it done. I still do things *her* way. It was a lesson well learned.

At Christmastime, Pepperell had a Christmas party at the Waldorf Astoria, the only time I was in that grand old place in my forty-six years in New York. I heard of that party long before it happened. "We get Lobster Thermidor," they exclaimed, which meant nothing to me as I had never heard of lobster.

There was a dress shop on 3rd Avenue with a seamstress, and they used me as their model. I was just the size they needed, and I loved doing it. If I modeled for them, then I could buy the dresses at a lower price, and that was great; no more hand-me-downs. I always looked nice going to work at Pepperell. It was a blessing for me, as I had the nicest clothes around for a fraction of their cost. In fact, I still have the blue glass tea set they gave me when I got married. My first party dress was a navy-blue satin, two-piece suit with a large rhinestone button. I bought a rhinestone pin in Woolworth's and earrings to match. I looked great. Even so, I was disappointed and sad with my looks, when the other women came to the party with long, black strapless gowns. The salesmen's wives all said their husbands liked me, and they were happy to meet me. In fact, I learned that one sales-man asked for me to be promoted to desk clerk for his depart-ment. Suddenly, I was glad I was me at that party, instead of a make-believe movie star.

I did borrow a long gown from Gertrude when Larry and I went to a night club in Manhattan much later. The firm needed me to be a switchboard operator right then, so I never got to be a sales representative's secretary. I enjoyed my work there, and was sad when I had to leave the company. I sent an announcement to Mr. Ferrini for the bulletin board when Bobby was born. I wanted to share my happiness with all of my many friends there.

I was the most proud when I got sworn in as a United States citizen in Lower Manhattan. It was 4th of July 1957, exactly five years after entering into the good old USA. This was the required waiting period for immigrants with permanent resident status to obtain citizenship. I went right back to Pepperell Manufacturing's sales office with my new certificate to show it off. They all were proud of me too. They complimented me on how nice I looked in my pink dress, white hat, and gloves. I was a real New York City Girl! I always knew I belonged here, but now I could prove it. Larry arrived here in 1949, as his family was sponsored by his father's sister, who came in 1927. He became a citizen after his service in the Marine Corps in December 1953, before we were married in February 1954.

Larry and I took a horse and buggy ride through Central Park hugging and kissing all the way. We had lunch at the Tavern On The Green restaurant by the lake in Central Park, and after that, we rented a paddle boat and paddled around on the lake. It was a wonderful day of celebration that I never will forget. I think my parents and Anna became citizens the same day. Freddy was too small then, and he became a citizen on our mother's papers on July 4th 1957.

I got a long letter of congratulations from Mr. Ferrini some days later, as he was not in the office that day. He, too, was proud of me. I was still thankful that he hired me that fateful day long ago, and told him so. He should be proud for taking a chance on me, with no experience in office work, and no references, except that employee's sister, Magda.

I became good friends with Lucy and Gertrude in the switchboard operating room at Pepperell that lasted a long time. Gertrude gave me a bassinet which my mom and sister outfitted with lace bedding. She also gave me a lot of baby clothes left over from her two children for my baby, Bobby. He was a big boy and outgrew his clothes fast. He looked so cute in the upscale jumpsuits when we went by bus to Upper Broadway, on the way to the Presbyterian Medical Center of Columbia University Hospital's allergy clinic to treat his eczema.

Gertrude advised me how to continue to have pre-natal care after I lost my job. She told me to go to the clinic at New York Hospital and explain my situation, which I did. They welcomed me as a clinic patient on a sliding scale fee, which we could afford. So, Bobby was born at New York Hospital, and delivered by Cornell University doctors. This was a blessing, as he was too large for natural birth, and after labor stopped he was not born yet. Luckily, his head was out, so that he did not suffocate. I had to wait for a specialist doctor to come and deliver him. Of course, I did not know any of this, only the young nurses that sat with me kept asking if I was okay, which I was. I saw them going out of the room shaking their heads, but did not know anything was wrong. This was my first experience having a baby and I didn't know any different.

I felt in good hands with the kind young nurses by my side. In the weeks after, I had a visit from home health nurses to check on my baby. Just one look around the clean apartment and the healthy thriving baby got me off their checklist. They were pleased at what they saw. They never checked on me again.

℃ℜ

Chapter Seventeen

From Miss to Mrs. to Mother (1954)

*I met famous Broadway and sports stars that stayed in my
hotel. It was the first time I saw a Broadway play.*

From Miss to Mrs. to mother all happened to me in 1954. Larry
and I married February 6, 1954, and Bobby was born October
21 of the same year. We three Buschbachers lived in Spanish
Harlem, New York

Larry left the Marine Corps late in 1953. He came to live with
his brother and sister-in-law in the Bronx. We had been writing
letters to each other for about a year, and he came to visit me
often from his post in Cherry Hill Navy Air Base, NC. He loved
the Marine Corps and North Carolina, where he spent his days
off on the beach. We talked about getting married when he visited. I told my parents our plans and they were delighted; they

loved Larry. My father said he would get him a job at the factory
where he worked; many Germans worked there, making parts
for airplanes for the government and they would love him. And
that's what happened. He was quick to learn, and he was a whiz
at measuring things as delicate as a fraction in accuracy. He soon
got promoted to the lab where only engineers were working.

Meanwhile, he and I looked for an apartment with the little money we had, and got a beautiful three-room place through the German language newspaper. I went to see it and fell in love with
it first. Soon Larry got to see it and loved it too. We signed a
lease. We painted the walls a mint green, had the parquet floors
scraped and refinished; it was a cute little home for us. My parents bought a kitchen table, my in-laws bought curtains and a
sofa to sleep on, as they planned to stay with us on their days off
from the Westchester's family where they worked. My brother-
in-law bought a new stove to replace the one that came with the
place. The old one was so full of grease that a fire could have
broken out as soon as we lit it. All that was left for us to do, was
to get married. We invited all our friends, who were new in the
country, along with Larry's family who came in the 1920s. It
was an exciting time in our lives. I rented my dress and Larry
rented his suit. I got a lot of advice from my friends at Pepperrell,
who were happy for me. All the household goods came together
at the wedding, as everyone bought pots and pans as gifts for us.
And Uncle Andreas Buschbacher's family gave us a beautiful set
of china that I loved then and still treasure.

My parent's best friends lived near them. They were a German
family, who owned a delicatessen shop on 2nd Avenue. Their
son was a little younger than me, and we socialized with each
other for many years. At a very young age, he married a sweet
little Polish girl. They had two children, and we remained good

Katharina & Lorenz
Buschbacher, Wedding day
NYC, Feb 6, 1954

friends even after we moved to Queens. His father came to the rescue the day I married Larry. We planned a reception in a local restaurant on 86th St., where Larry and I went dancing every chance we had. The Rhineland was its name. We loved the band, and were told their live music from upstairs could be piped into the basement room for our reception. We could not afford to rent the restaurant and the band, so the basement room would have to do. Our marriage ceremony was held at St. Joseph's Catholic Church on 86th Street at the corner of York Avenue. We had no car, so we made sure everything was within walking distance. It was close to the 86th Street subway stop for our guests too, since most new immigrants had no car. About 50 people attended as wedding guests. We enjoyed a nice German dinner, which started with soup. When the band played upstairs, the static was so bad over the speakers that we couldn't enjoy anything. My friend's father, Mr. Bauer, went home to get his Victrola and his German records, and he played dancing music for our wedding feast. He saved the day!

Our address, 561 West 140 Street, was the first building in a row of six-storey buildings right after the store's loading zone facing Broadway. The row of houses ended with a park and playground for young children. The front door was a heavy glass door, leading to a marble foyer, and another set of full-length, glass double-doors leading to the lobby, which also was all marble. The curved staircase going up six floors was marble too, with a brass railing, and a wall of brass mailboxes under the staircase. Ours was the first apartment on the left, as you entered the lobby. There was one more apartment on the left, and one on the right next to the front door. No children lived in this house; we were all working adults. This building was much nicer than the six-storey building my parents took care of on 83rd St. The superintendent's apartment was under our apartment in a daylight basement—not a dungeon like my parents had. I felt sorry for the superintendent, as he had to clean all this marble and brass. I know how that was, as Anne and I had the job of washing down the staircase every Saturday, and polishing the brass mailboxes and glass doors of the building that my parents took care of.

As soon as we could we bought a radio, on which we could listen to a German program every day telling us where to shop, where we could worship, and everything else that German-speaking immigrants needed to know to ease us into our new culture. Ilse Wagner, the announcer, spoke perfect German. She knew which stores catered to new immigrants with their merchandise, and also possibly a German speaking sales person. This radio station in the 1950/60, (W.O.R. I think was the name) had other foreign-language programs for new immigrants as well.

Larry was able to get a ride to the factory in Queens from a man that lived in the Bronx.   I could take the subway train to work on Broadway on 139th Street. Everything worked out very well. Larry and I were happy there.

After I had to leave Pepperell because I was pregnant, I worked in the local bakery from 6:00 pm to 10:00 pm every night, which I continued even after the baby was born. Larry got home very punctually at 6:00 pm, and I made it in a few minutes to the bakery. I had my baby fed and ready for bed, and also Larry's supper on the stove. He played with his little boy, and both went to sleep before I got home every night. I remember one night, I checked on my baby when I got home, and had the shock of my life, as he had a bandage wrapped around his head. I woke up Larry and the baby to look at his head. Larry said he fell and hit his head. When I removed the bandage and saw that there was no blood, only a little bump on his forehead, I was relieved.

Now, I thought, it was time to do something else for work. I needed to be home with my family. I looked in the newspaper for jobs, and was so surprised to read "Catholics need not apply" and other discriminating remarks. This was before I knew there were separate water fountains and entrances for some of our citizens. I never knew that about my new country. I thought as a DP, I was discriminated against, but not in my own country. This was a shock to me.

A displaced person in Austria could only work as a servant, or on farms, or helping with cleaning the rubble away from the bombed-out buildings. Also, after age 14, you were not allowed to receive any more education. But we entered the same door to a building.

Soon, I was able to get a more suitable job making more money. I became the relief cashier in the Paramount Hotel on 46th Street, in the theatre district of Manhattan. This worked out very well,

Katharina & Robert Buschbacher
Lunchtime at home
W 140 St., NY, 1954

since my parents had their house now in Astoria. I took the subway train with my baby and laundry to my mother in Astoria on Wednesday afternoon, and worked Wednesday night. Then, I went home to sleep a few hours, changed my clothes, and was back at work at 7:00 am in the hotel on Thursday. I then went back to my mother's to pick up my baby and my clean laundry. I would have a good dinner and enough left over for a doggy bag for my husband and then go home till the next week, when we did this all over again. It worked out for several years. Sometimes, I stayed over to shop with Mom and Anne on Steinway Street. It was a special shopping area with prices cheaper than department store.

I met famous Broadway and sports stars that stayed in my hotel. It was the first time I saw a Broadway play. I was invited by Gwen Verden, the star of the show, *Damn Yankees*. Both Larry and I were in awe of this show. Larry could relate especially well, as it was about the New York Yankees baseball team, which he followed along with the Mets.

Soon, Larry and I were able to buy a car. It was green with white stripes on each side, 1956 Chevy Impala. He could then meet us at my parents after work, where we had dinner and went home in style with our little boy and clean laundry. My brother, Freddy, was in the local Catholic elementary school. He had great fun playing with his two-year-old nephew, Bobby. My sister, Anna, was also still at home with our parents. So, my little boy had plenty of TLC, and did not miss his parents much during those two days.

My mother had a garden right out the back door of their basement apartment, with fresh vegetables and beautiful flowers. My father fixed up one apartment after the other to rent. This three-family house, which was so run-down when they bought it, became the showcase of the neighborhood when he had finished with it.

Dad and Larry continued to work in the tool-and-die-making shop until it closed after many years. Larry and I lived in our apartment until 1958. We were happy there. Riverside Drive was just two blocks east, with a beautiful grassy walkway and benches next to the Hudson River. It was cool in summer, and many ladies with baby carriages walked there every day, like me. Later, Bobby and I walked along Broadway every day enjoying the store-front windows, and making friends with the store keepers. We had friends, and went to dances on Saturday nights, while one of our mothers would take care of Bobby. He was a delight to have. It was a memorable time for all of us.

My family had a church sponsor from Catholic Charities, who was a farmer in Iowa. We stayed in New York because, by the time we arrived, he no longer needed us. It was a blessing in disguise. I loved living in New York City. I don't know if I would have liked Iowa. I am glad our sponsorship was no longer valid, and we did not have to go there to fulfill our duty on their farm for year. I could, and did, expand my love of the arts.

In Manhattan, there were always new things to explore. In Far Rockaway, the beach was the jewel; in Manhattan, it was Broadway. Riverside Drive was for strolling and enjoying the Hudson River waterfront, which was different from Broadway, but also very special.

I was always asked to show the beach and Broadway to our visitors from Germany and Austria; even to some of our countrymen from other parts of the United States and Canada. It was the time for finding old friends from home and comparing our new life in our new homelands. Neither the Bachert nor Buschbacher families in Manhattan were familiar with our new home like I was. Nobody in either family knew and loved these places like I did.

I took my children to Radio City Music Hall for every holiday show. We did not have enough money sometimes, but I figured out how we could do it anyway. We entered the theater at 11:00 am, when tickets were the cheapest. We saw the closing show of the Rockettes, and then went downstairs where there were plush red velvet seats and marble floors. We were comfortable there and waited for the new program to start at 1:00 pm. I made sandwiches at home, so we ate lunch, played a game, and time went by quickly. I and my children especially liked to window shop on Fifth Avenue at Christmastime. FAO Schwarz, Macys, Bloomingdales, and some other stores had outstanding window decorations, sometimes with moving mannequins, and falling snow. It was a highlight of the day to visit to the city. At night, we went with Larry in the car, and sometimes with the grand-parents too, to see the Rockefeller Christmas Tree, and to St Pat-rick's Cathedral, which always had a beautiful manger scene on display. We continued these visits with our college age children, when they came home for Christmas. Larry always expected them home for Christmas, no matter where they were the rest of the year. Family get-togethers at holidays were always important to our family, then and even now, we continue the tradition. I always say that my son, Bobby, learned from the cracks on the sidewalk in Manhattan, where he was born and lived to age four. We had no money for toys, but we studied the shop windows as we walked past every day. He always noticed what was new. So, I know even poor children can learn, if they are exposed to the world around them and talked to about it all. I made it my life's work to continue that philosophy, by volunteering in read-ing programs with children of all ages.

We enjoyed taking rides into the country on weekends. We packed lunch and had a picnic winter or summer. We watched the ski jumps on Bear Mountain all winter. Our apartment building was broken into several times, but never our place. We had a friend on the sixth floor whose kitchen window was broken into at least once a month. It seemed the robbers came from the neighboring building and down the roof on a rope. One Sunday, we packed the car in front of our apartment window. Larry leaned the sled against the car to come in and get the rest of us. When we got outside, the sled was gone. Another thing that happened was, one day on our walk, I suspected a man was following me. I stopped in stores to check this out. Yes, each time I came out, that man was leaning against a lamppost, and when I walked on, so did he. I was convinced this man was following me. I went into the laundromat that was run by a young couple who knew me. I told them that a man was following me. This friend went outside to look for himself, and sure enough, that man was still leaning against a lamp pole, looking at a newspaper every time my friend looked outside. After a long time, as this man was still there, the proprietor called the police. They came and asked that man if he was following me. Of course, he said he was not following anybody and left. I went home, looking around me, scared. It was time to get out of the city.

CR

Chapter Eighteen

Moving to Howard Beach (1958)

...we lived there for 46 years.
Debbie called it, The Gingerbread House...

We looked for a house, and the further away from Manhattan you went, the cheaper they got. We had a little money, and were able to borrow the rest from our parents to make a down payment on a five-year-old house, ready to move in to. We had no money for curtains, rugs or anything else. My mother made curtains for all windows, gave us their bed for Bobby, who had been in a crib till now. We made do with that. We loved living in our own house. So, we bought our house at 158-43 83rd Street Howard Beach, Queens, NY.

The community of Howard Beach then was small and new. It was a bedroom community of Manhattan. The major road to the ocean divided the old town with larger estate type homes, and the new section created after WWII. These Cape-style homes were built in former swampland, and were supported by steel poles driven deep into the muck. The 40 x 100-foot and 60 x 100-foot lots were organized in rows from 156th to 159th Avenues and Cross Bay Boulevard to 83rd Street.

The people who lived there were exactly the kind of people we wanted for our neighbors. They were young and just starting out, as we were. Larry was a proud Marine, and most neighbors were former GIs. Some even were WWII veterans. Many worked for New York City as police and firemen. We wanted young families for neighbors, as we wanted a second child now. We wanted to have a great place for our children to grow up, with other children of outstanding, working-class citizens like us around. We found this in Howard Beach. We blended well and our children had many friends. It was a great place to raise a family. It was a long train ride to Manhattan, and a short bus ride to Ozone Park, where the subway stop was.

I worked for 30 years at the elementary school there. Later, it was also would be only a half hour car ride to Larry's Liquor Store on Hillside Avenue in Jamaica Estates. The tool and die factory was sold and moved to Connecticut. We took a trip to Connecticut to see where it had moved to in Bridgeport. The company changed its name to Pall Electronics, and Larry was invited to work for them. We both did not like Bridgeport, Connecticut. We had a big debate whether he should take the job or not. Finally, Larry decided to follow his dream of owning his own business. In Indjija, he was an apprentice in a retail store, and he always dreamed of having his own store some day.

He took a chance on a run-down liquor store, and made it big. It was a good thing it was close to home, as he worked 80 hours a week at first. A half hour car ride to Jamaica was doable. Larry had his store for over 30 years. He was a successful business man. I can only imagine what he would have achieved, had he had the opportunity to gain a higher education.

Howard Beach was also just a half hour or less to Rockaway Beach and Jamaica Bay for exploring marine life. We had beautiful back yard with shade trees, flowers, and an apple tree that gave us apples for pancakes and lunch. Larry planted peppers and tomatoes to cook with too. Later, we had a large swimming pool. It was the hang out place for friends and family all summer, and we lived there for 46 years. Debbie called it, "The Gingerbread House." It had white aluminum siding, with window boxes always filled with red geraniums. The black shutters gave it class. Debbie was born in that house, grew up and got married there. We always had Christmas at our house. Larry told his children, "Wherever you may be, come Christmas, we expect you to be home with the family." This is what we always did. We all spent our last Christmas there without some family members, who were no longer with us, or had moved to Florida. We were ready to follow them there in April 1995.

Larry died there in 2003. Rest in peace, Larry. I am proud to say he rests at Arlington National Cemetery, still a proud Marine —Sargent Lorenz Buschbacher. The memories will always stay on in our hearts, with the family, and the Boy Scouts of Howard Beach, Troop 214.

Friends Old and New

Gertrude and John were lifelong friends. They had a long marriage with two grown children: One in college and one in high school. When we bought our house in Howard Beach, they often came for the weekend. John worked for the railroad, transporting apples and other fruit from upstate New York. He had access to boxes of over-ripe fruit the vendors left on the train or just gave away, as it was not saleable in their stores. John and Gertrude brought it to us. Gertrude and I made fruit salad, and there was a lot for us to enjoy during the week as well.

Gertrude still worked at Pepperell for a while, but retired shortly after John retired from the railroad. Gertrude and I reminisced about my time working with her, as a switchboard operator in that huge corner office with no windows. It was a scary place with the huge switch board across the back wall, and many different-colored wires hanging down from it. In this little private room, we knew all the gossip about all the salesmen and their secretaries.

Gertrude and John admired me for teaching my son the alphabet and other kindergarten stuff. He was four years old by the time we had enough money for a down payment on a house in the suburbs. If we were rich, he would have had a governess to teach him, so I patterned myself after that philosophy. I thought my children should have a better education then I had. I watched the governesses on Broadway, walking their charges on Riverside Drive. My son learned from the cracks on the sidewalk on Broadway and the store windows we checked out every day. An education will give them a better life I thought. Gertrude looked at the schedule I had for the week and was always proud of what I did. Her son was in college, and her daughter on the way to college. Gertrud never drove a car, and when John passed away, it was too much for her to come to Howard Beach by subway train, as it took over two hours from far away Bronx. We unfortunately drifted apart, but, I treasure those memories in my heart. She was my mentor and long-time friend.

Our second child, Debbie Anne, was born in Howard Beach in 1960. My children had many friends in Howard Beach, as they grew up. Larry and I started speaking English with each other, as we wanted to be just as all-American as possible, for our children's sake. We reserved Wednesday as German day for language and food. Our parents preferred to speak in our Austrian/Hungarian dialect when we had family get-togethers, which was frequently, and especially on holidays.

Robert (6) & Debbie Anne (3 mo) Buschbacher Howard Beach, 1961

Our neighbors were all young and just starting out, but they were a little older than we were. It was a good fit for us, as well as our children. None of us had much money, and we got together to celebrate holidays or birthdays in each other's houses. We often hosted these gatherings, as we had a finished basement with built-in benches all around, and plenty of room for dancing to our favorite records. The children got together in another house, with the older ones watching the younger ones. Parents checked on them often, and brought food. It was a great life. The camaraderie among the neighbors, friends, and our children was remarkable, never a harsh word was spoken. We loved our house and we loved our neighbors in Howard Beach. It was a quiet, restful place. It was far from everywhere, and we had to bus to the next town of Ozone Park, where we could then take a subway line to Manhattan, via Brooklyn. Or

we could walk a good half-hour to Old Howard Beach to get the
elevated subway line to nearby East New York, Brooklyn. I had
to walk to Cross Bay Boulevard to shop in the only store we had,
an A&P. It was not easy getting the groceries home with baby,
Debbie, in her carriage. Bobby was by then in elementary school
in PS 63, in Ozone Park.

I wanted to learn how to drive, so I could shop in the evening,
but Larry told me it was impossible to pay for the insurance,
when more than one person drove a car. So, I kept on walking
everywhere. Sometimes, a kind school-bus driver let me and my
little girl ride to school when they picked up Bobby, as I was
always volunteering on several projects the Parent Teacher organization undertook.

I became interested in the educational system, as I had very little
education myself. I was going to do everything in my power to
see that my children got the best education available. I became
very active, and was an elected officer in the Parent Teacher As-
sociation. I remember the first time I had to address a meeting,
my knees were shaking. Many times, Debbie slept behind the
stage in the auditorium at PS 63, as we waited for the afternoon
school bus to take us home. More and more, my teacher instinct
raised its head. I was still bemoaning the fact that I could not go
to school in Austria after age fourteen. I became a volunteer to
help children with reading, I checked kids for head lice, I conducted hearing and vision checks, etc. All things that could be
done during the school day. I even led fundraisers, such as bake
sales, book drives, and more. I had no transportation, other than
kind school bus drivers, or other mothers who had a car for the
day. It was not common in those days for families to have two
cars. Many of my neighbor's children went to Catholic school
in old Howard Beach, and they had no connection with the pub-

lic-school system. As my neighborhood grew, two new schools were built locally; an elementary school in Howard Beach, just in time for my daughter to start kindergarten. The second school, between Howard Beach and Ozone Park, was a middle school. PS 63 was a kindergarten to eighth grade school, up till then, but Robert Goddard Junior High School received students after they graduated elementary school in 6th grade, and that provided for lots of room to accept black students from nearby Jamaica, Queens in the open enrollment system.

Since, I was in school so much, the principal asked me if I would take on the job of coordinating the bus service for the open-enrollment students. They came from the overcrowded schools in Jamaica. I said yes. It gave me a two-hour, paid job, among all other volunteer work I did there. I had to apply to the city of New York, get fingerprinted, and had a chest x-ray, before I was approved to be a city employee. I was very happy, as I no longer had to go to the local doctor's office, where I also worked two nights a week.

I loved the new job, but getting to school every day was a problem. I had to get a ride or hire a car service for a while. Soon, a friendly neighbor, Joe Suess, was selling his old Buick for very little money. *Rosie* was his pride and joy, but the body was rusted. He tinkered with the engine every day, and it ticked like a clock. He told me if I wanted it, he would maintain it. This was a blessing, as I needed a mentor, but he did not teach me to drive. Larry said he would not have anything to do with the situation. If I wanted to drive, I had better get to a credited driving school. I thought he was right; I'd better learn from a professional. So, I went to driving school, learned to drive, bought Rosie, and was on my own. The floor was rusted out, but Rosie's body looked like new. Larry, or Joe, I don't remember who, put some boards in the floor across the back, so the children's feet did not come through—we had no seat belts back then. But, I only drove through the neighborhood, and went slowly. It was a pleasure to get my groceries home with no problems. Debbie went to the library for story hour, while I did my shopping. It all worked out well.

Larry was working hard to build his retail business, Larry's Liquors. He worked from 9:00 am to 9:00 pm every weekday, and 9:00 am to 11:00 pm on weekends. On Saturdays, I opened the store to let him sleep late. My father came on the subway to sit with me so I would not be alone because of hold-ups. Then I drove him home and had dinner with my parents. Mom made a dinner plate for Larry so I did not have to cook for him. We both grew in various ways.   My Union was so helpful to me, because they gave courses for members to better themselves. I took a course every Saturday once Larry had an assistant in the store. Spanish, English as a second language, math, and typing. Free education was a gift to me, and I took advantage of it all. They had a writing class in Queens General Hospital for nurses' aides. I took that too, as I had a car and could get myself there on my own after school. I needed to learn to write also.

At that time, the School for Language and Hearing-Impaired Children (SLIC) was looking for a place in Queens to expand the services for Queens's children. The Deaf School in Queens did not take hearing impaired children, as they were not deaf. So, these children had to travel to Manhattan every day to the main school. At our school, the whole fourth floor became empty after the junior high was built. We had a home economics kitchen, and a woodworking shop for the former 8th graders. This now became useful for the handicapped children that moved in. The special education coordinator asked for help from our principal.

I had only part-time work, so I volunteered for it. I became the administrative assistant to the SLIC Coordinator for 12 years, and we are lifetime friends. She is the one who suggested I get my general education diploma (GED) and go to college. I was surprised this was even possible. My children were getting bigger, my husband worked night and day, so it was an easy decision to make. I took a prep course from my Union DC 37, took the test, passed, and went on to college. It was a chance for me to realize my dream to become a teacher. Only in America did I have this chance. I am forever grateful to my new homeland.

I grew in different ways too. When I learned about the slaughter of whales, I protested with the Greenpeace Organization to help stop it. I was made aware of people in our own country were being treated as second-class citizens, even though they were born here. So, we marched and marched, and wrote letters to politicians to rectify the situation. Having never left New York since arriving in 1952, I was not aware of that until the Civil Rights movement started in the 1960s. My son had a friend from high school, who went to Cornell University—an Ivy League school that my son also attended. He happened to be black, and they were roommates there. My family never saw color; only the person's values when we met somebody.

My best and lifelong friend, from New York, whom I met when I worked with the language and hearing-impaired children, happens to be black. She, her husband, and some neighbors, came to buy some of our furniture when we left New York, to retire in Florida in 1995. We are still, and always will be, friends. My best friend in my retirement community in Florida also happens to be black. When I became President of the General Federation Woman's Club in Florida, I asked her to join and be my secretary. She was the first black woman to join that club, and she is

still there, having been a president twice, and is still a District
4 officer in Florida. My husband, our children and I never saw
color in people, only character.

My job as educational associate to teach reading was my most
rewarding job at PS 63. I am still a dues-paying member of the
United Federation of Teachers even in retirement. I have some
correspondence from the young adults, who appreciated my help
when they needed it as children. I am proud of my own children;
they gave me nothing but happiness, as they always stand out in
everything they do. Larry and I were always there to cheer them
on, and to stand proudly with them, as they were honored for
their achievements, which were many.

Graduating with honors from high school, Bobby was valedicto-
rian. He received a full tuition scholarship to St John's University in Queens, which he turned down for a partial scholarship
to Cornell University. Debbie was a Camp Fire Girl. My son
was the first Eagle Scout at age fourteen for Troup 214. Debbie
obtained a scholarship into Florida Atlantic University. Living in
New York was a blessing; the opportunities there were all welcome, like the All-Borough Band for Bobby, who played alto
saxophone. Leonard Bernstein was conductor. Debbie played
the flute in her school band. Bobby played his alto saxophone in
the Howard Beach Voluntary Firemen Band. They had march-
ing competitions every Saturday night in different Long Island
towns with Volunteer Fire departments. They often won. Luckily, I had a new Nissan Sentra car, which Larry bought me after
he saw that I was serious about driving. Debbie and I took Bobby
to these festivals and parades on Long Island every Saturday in
summer. Debbie and I traveled two hours each way on the subway to the Bronx Zoo for Bobby to have a free week of summer
camp there. When he came to meet us at the end of his days, his

eyes lit up like light bulbs, when he told us what they did each day. "Oh, Mom, we got to feed the snakes today!" His eyes were as big as baseballs, and that made it all worthwhile. When these invitations came to my school, my friends asked if I was crazy to go all that way. I said no. I value the chance for free education when it is offered. While Bobby was at camp, Debbie and I got to know every animal and its habitat. We knew when to go to the rainforest building for the thunderstorm. I could not have paid for these opportunities for all the gold in China. I valued them and still do value education in all forms. Don't be too lazy to take advantage of it.

As Camp Fire leaders, we were able to use the girl scout camp for a week in Rhode Island. Yes, you guessed it, Mrs. Mosler and I took our girls to Rhode Island for a week, so they could experience a summer camp. We had to clean out the cobwebs and get the cabins ready for summer. It was a wonderful experience for our city girls to fish and hike. We learned about trees and wildflowers, which I still think of when, on a rare occasion, I see a Lady Slipper or a Pitcher plant on my walks in the woods of North Carolina.

We both enjoyed our house in Howard Beach. We loved seeing our children grow there. We lived close to Jamaica Bay, where our kids went wading to check out the clams and horse shoe crabs. When they got older, they went to Rockaway Beach on the Atlantic Ocean to swim. I often think of the poem written on the brick wall in Rockaway's Playland, where my children rode their first roller-coaster, and its historic merry go round. As you entered Playland, it was written on the wall, "The most beautiful music in the world is the sound of children's laughter." I find that to be still true today.

Those happy years will always live on in the hearts of our family. My sister's three children spent many summers with us. My parents and I went all over with them too. I read the stories at night, but the youngest boy did not like many of the library books I had, he preferred the stories I made up. He often asked to repeat a certain story, and if I made a mistake as I did not remember it well enough, he said, "Aunt Katie, you should write this down." Family Christmas dinners were held in our house, as well. My sister was Jewish, and did not celebrate Christmas anymore. When she wanted to get married to Bernard, a Jew. The priest in her church urged her to change her mind. After much ado, she decided to get married in Bernard's Jewish religion, as she wanted God's blessing of their bond.

After several years of marriage and raising her daughter and two boys in the Jewish tradition, she decided to become Jewish herself. My sister and her husband have been happily married for 51 years. She feels at home in her Jewish faith. She is valued as a contributing member of the sisterhood, and is honored for the many things she does there. The Bachert family is still as close knit as ever. We made an adjustment to accommodate Anne's new religion. Anne and Bernard will now only host the family Thanksgiving feast in Connecticut where they lived then. Katie and Larry host the Christmas get-together, as Larry's family, the Buschbachers, his parents and his brother, Valentine, with his family, are to be a part of this also. Anne's children had the best of both worlds, because they celebrated Hanukkah at home, then Christmas with their Mom's family. We had a ping-pong table in the basement, which became the dinner table at Christmas, as my family (the Bacherts) and Larry's family (the Buschbachers) grew. In both families, our children were our pride and joy. They were lucky to grow up with four grandparents, and to learn a little of their ancestral culture. We always referred to *home,* when we spoke of Indjija.

I am the oldest in my family, and my husband Larry—or Lenz, as he was called by his parents, was the youngest. We too learned from our parents as to how life was for them in Indjija. In summers, family get-togethers were in our house as we had a big yard with a swimming pool, a brick fireplace for cooking our barbeque dinners. Both Omas brought strudel and torte for dessert. Birthdays, school graduations, First Holy Communion and Confirmations, all took place there.

Debbie said she would only get married from our house, if I removed the plastic slipcovers from the plush velvet couch and chairs in the living room. This was okay, as now the family was smaller and the children were bigger, so it was safe to show off the gold plush fabric on the Spanish wooden chairs. A huge portrait of a Flamenco dancer, which Larry and I brought home from Spain, hung over these chairs. This room was my pride and joy. So, when Debbie and Jeff got married in 1988, it was also the gathering place for our new family members: Jeff's family from Ohio. Debbie and Jeff moved to Texas, where they still live with their two grown children. My sister, with her family live in Florida. My brother, Fred, was serving in the US Army in Vietnam. When he left the military, he became a police officer in Florida. He settled in with my sister and brother-in-law until he married. My son, Bobby, was working for the World Wildlife Fund in Brazil, where he married Margareth, and where his son Thomas Jefferson was born. Howard Beach has changed for many of our neighbors too. Job-wise, family-wise, the close-knit Howard Beach family drifted apart after 46 years, but the memories will always stay in our hearts.

❧

Reflections on Family

Parents

(Top row) Valentin, Katharina, Lorenz, Else (Sitting) Rosina & Lorenz Buschbacher
Wedding day, Feb 6, 1954

In 1961, Larry's parents, Rosie and Lorenz Buschbacher retired to the house they bought on 36th Street in Astoria, just one street away from Steinway Street. His parents worked as domestics in a Jewish household, where they did not need to know the English language. It was good for them, as they were older, and only had 10 or 12 years to work till they retired. They also got a sizable chunk of money from the German government in reparation for the land, house, and saddlery business, they lost in Yugoslavia in the war.

Larry was from my hometown of Indjija. My father-in-law's sister and her husband, Anna and Wendel, in Walden, NY, sponsored them, and sent them tickets for the ocean liner, *Italia,* from Genoa, Italy.

All they had to do was take a train from Stuttgart, Germany, to Italy to get on the ship to America. Larry was the ping-pong champion on the *Italia* during that voyage. He was always athletic, he even played soccer for the Marine Corps in North Carolina.

Katharina & Lorenz Buschabcher hug Maria Bachert at 23rd St., Astoria, NY, circa 1958

Around 1960, my parents had a few thousand dollars saved up as a down payment for an old, three-family house in Queens. The sellers were Serbians, who immigrated to America early in the 1920s and trusted my parents to hold the mortgage, as my parents were not eligible for a loan from the bank. Dad did all the renovation himself, moving from one apartment in the house to another, all the while living in the day-lit basement, which had a back door to the garden that my mother loved.

The housing market in New York rose to great heights by the time my parents wanted to retire in 1988. The sale of their house in Queens helped sustain them well in retirement. Because we lived in Austria when The Great War ended, they got no compensation for the house and property they lost in Yugoslavia. My father had also paid union dues in three countries while living and working there. My mom received a lifetime pension and health benefits for the many years she worked cleaning offices in the city's financial district, which was a great help to them in their retirement years. Mom and Dad loved the Sunshine State. They had to deal with bad weather conditions often during the New York winters. My father chopped the ice from the steps leading into their house, as they were responsible for the safety of their tenants, and they took that job seriously.

Out of Yugoslavia, Austria and the good old USA, the United States was the only country he and Mom collected a pension from. As much as we loved them, the old countries were not kind to my parents in the end. They could not afford to be.

My parents were generous people. The Catholic churches in New York (Astoria) and in Jacksonville, Florida where they worshipped, have plaques on the walls with their names on them, commemorating them as valued members. They never forgot how well they fared in life, even considering all the trouble they had along the way. They were always thankful to the Lord above. They made many charitable donations to religious organizations, mostly to help children. Mother knew that there were always a great many children, who needed help. My Mother always thought the Blessed Mother was keeping her safe, as she had had a very sad childhood.

When my mother, Maria Brucker, was two years old, her own mother died in childbirth. My grandmother's name was Katharina Gartner Brucker. I am her namesake. My mother had no contact with her mother's family. She had a stepmother, who was married to a man who drank too much; my maternal grandfather, Johann Brucker. Her stepmother eventually took her two biological children, and left the home of this drunk, leaving his own daughter behind. My mother had to tend to him, and fend for herself from a very young age. Only the Blessed Mother could help get her through those years. She always considered the Blessed Mother was her mother too. My mother went to work with her father on construction sites at eight or nine years old. She had only three years of schooling, which was not all that uncommon. It was only important to go to school to learn to read and write. Hard work was what was needed in those days, in the hinterlands of Yugoslavia. There was a Hungarian school to go to after attending four years of elementary school, but most children of farming families were needed in the fields, as soon as they were able to help. Many children from the farms far outside town never went to school, as it was not possible to get there.

Of course, nobody wanted to learn Hungarian after the First World War, as the boundaries changed from Hungary to Yugo-slavia. The Serbian King did not care about educating his newly acquired people. My mother always sent me to school, as she re-alized a complete, basic education was important. She also sent me to visit her stepfamily during my school vacation at a very young age, even though she did not have a fondness for them. They lived in Semlin, a suburb of Belgrade. It was a mixed town of Serbians, Croatians, and Germans, I think. They were kind to me, and I did not have to work for them, just visit. My mother always valued family ties and they honored that. She kept our family close together all her life. She wanted her stepfamily to know her children, and us to know them. We spent many nice summers together, before the war in1942. We went to Belgrade to the theatre and just spent time together. My mother's half-sister, Lissi, and half-brother, Franz, never married. They saw a lot of hardship between their parents I guess, which discouraged them.

I met other Brucker family members while I was in Semlin. My maternal grandfather's two sisters lived there. Aunt Rosie and her husband were very nice to me. The other sister was an actress in Belgrade, and I hardly ever saw her, except in her plays. Her name was Resca, a Serbian endearment for the name, Theresia. I don't think she was married. My mother did not feel a part of that family, her father lived with us mostly. He and his son, Franz Brucker, went to live and work in Germany for a few years under Hitler's *Heim ins Reich* (coming home) program. Hitler encouraged all German-speaking people in the outside of Germany to move back to the Vaterland.

Mom told me her parents would ask her, "Who do you love more?" And when she answered, "Dad," her stepmother would take it out on her the rest of the week. When she said, "Mom," her father would hit her. She was always in the middle of their fights, and got pushed around like a chess pawn. Her strong faith in God, and especially the Blessed Mother, kept her going. That is why Anna, Freddy, and I, were so important to her. Family was everything to her, especially her children. She told us about the two children she lost; my brother Franzi, as a baby, and my sister, Maria, a toddler. She missed them. She made sure we got together every Christmas and other holidays, and as much as was possible at other times of the year. But especially Christmas, that was a must. I remember when she lived in the retirement community of the Pines of Mandarin, she made ravioli for her grandchildren. I said, "Mom we can buy that." She said, "No, not with meat filling. I make few at a time, then put them in the freezer until I have enough. I ask Anne to make the sauce and invite my grandchildren for dinner." She lived to be 95 years old.

Siblings

Freddy went to Immaculate Conception School in Astoria and Long Island City High School. Then to Vietnam with the US Army. After he left the military, he went to UNF in Jacksonville, Florida, and was the first of our family to graduate from college. He was a police officer in Florida for over 20 years. Then, he retired to South Carolina and became the post master in his new home town. He built a house on a mountain top he calls Fred's Summit. He still lives there.

(Standing) Bernard, Anne De Paul, Rosina,
Lorenz, Katharina Buschbacher, (Sitting)
Franz, Maria, Brenda & Alfred Bachert
Debbie & Jeff's wedding, Long Island, NY
July 9, 1988

Anna changed her name to the American version, she is now Anne. She did so well in Julia Richmond High School that the guidance counselor came to the house to speak to my parents to encourage them to let her go to college. But my parents said, "No. Let her learn how to work. That's how you get ahead in life." That was the old country mentality; working with your hands was the best thing you could do. They both did well by working hard all their lives, and thought it best for Anne too. She soon got married and moved to Connecticut with her new husband, a doctor of dentistry, Bernard De Paul. They soon moved to Florida, where he opened his practice and where Anne worked too. They celebrated their 51st wedding anniversary in 2017. They still live in Florida with their three grown children.

Twice Blessed with Love

The year 2003 was the worst year of my adult life.

Larry and I enjoyed our retirement in Florida's beach community with other newcomers through the Newcomers' Club. This club grew so rapidly, that after two years, we had to leave. We had such a close-knit friendship established there, and did not want to break up this relationship. I became the founding president of the Newcomers Alumna Club, and we continued the social events we enjoyed with our friends.

Larry and I traveled all over the world. We went back to our birth place, Indjija. Larry's house was now a hotel, but his grandmother's house was intact. It was just as he remembered it, with the same lace curtains on the windows, and the missing wooden slat in the back fence that he took out to retrieve his soccer ball. My house had a second-story, the walnut tree and pear tree were gone, and so was my mother's vegetable garden where another house now stood.

We both volunteered a lot in our spare time. We did some things together, like ushering in the Historic Florida Theatre, and volunteering at the Beaches Fine Arts Triathlon. Some things we did separately. My favorite was volunteering with children in the Neptune Beach Elementary School, and with the school children at the Cummer Fine Arts Museum. I had first and second grade every week. The Jacksonville Zoo was my Saturday project. I was an Exhibition Attendant at the Native Florida exhibit and the African Welt. I took my mother, at age 94, with me, because she loved animals all her life. I put her on the train to see the big animals, while I did lecturing at my posts. Then, we made the rounds to some other places like the koala bears, and other Australian animals connected to the bird-feeding station. In 2001, I had the honor of being named Volunteer of the Year for the Jacksonville Beaches Community.

This all came crashing down on me when Larry passed away, suddenly, on May 4, 2003. My Mom died soon after, on August 29, 2003.

Our friends and neighbors, Carol and Tom De Kay, left Florida for North Carolina where they were summer residents for 20 years. Carol passed away there on April 15, 2003.

Tom and I consoled each other long-distance on the phone for two years. He called me on Tuesday evenings, and we talked for a long time. It was a comfort to both of us, as we knew each other's spouses, and knew the great loss we both suffered. Tom and Carol were married 52 years, Larry and I, 49 years.

I spent the summer of 2005 in Brazil with my son and his family. Margareth, my daughter-in-law, is from there, and her family was warm and welcoming. There, the telephone company added another digit to the existing phone number, which made it difficult for Tom to call me. When he finally got through in late July, he was so glad to talk to me again, and asked me to marry him. He promised me 10 good years. I accepted his proposal, as I missed him too. We got engaged in August 2005, when I returned from Brazil. We traveled back and forth from his house to mine, until we decided to make ourselves into one family, with one home.

Tom & Katie De Kay,
Wedding day
Jacksonville Beach, FL,
Jan. 18, 2007

We got married, I sold my house, and moved to North Carolina. I never thought I could love it here so much, as it is rural and I am a New York City girl. But Tom had the best answer, he said, "We don't have to live in the big city, we can travel to it." So, we traveled to the Peace Center in Greenville, having season tickets to the Master Works, just like we had in Jacksonville for all the years we lived there. Now, the Hendersonville Symphony has a nice place for their concerts in the Community College Media Building, and we subscribe there too. Flat Rock Theatre is North Carolina's State Theatre, and is just minutes from our house and I have season tickets there as well.

The nature here is very inspiring for writing poetry and short stories, just by watching humming birds, and all kinds of wild animals walking down the street. Some months we have a black bear in residence in our wooded back yard. Many artists live and work here. Every little historic town has art festivals and craft fairs. The hills are alive with music of all kinds. Tom's favorite was blue grass. I never heard it before, but besides classical, it is my favorite now also. Most every restaurant has live music here. Fine dining is everywhere. Now, this New York girl loves the country in Western North Carolina. My friends, and the women's clubs I belong to, are retirees from elsewhere in the country, and they too love it here. Tom and I have traveled somewhere special every year.

This year, on our cruise to Central America and Mexico, Tom had a heart attack on the ship's stop in Honduras. My forever friend in New York sent her cousin, who has a business at Coxen Hole, Honduras, to stay with me at the hospital that day. Later that night, her husband, nephew, and his wife came also, all speaking English. I was so grateful not to be alone in a foreign country under these circumstances. We airlifted him to Florida, where he passed away. I am forever thankful to the doctor in Honduras, who kept him alive long enough to come home to die in the country he loved, and fought for in WWII.

His last day on the ship was very special to him. Every ship has a veteran's gathering, but on this one he was the only WWII veteran. People came to us at the dinner table to take a picture with him.

He asked, "Why do you want my picture?" They answered, "You are a celebrity on this ship!" He said, "I don't need any glory, I just did my job." But I know he loved the recognition, he smiled all day.

Tom was a people-person, he talked to all who would listen. He was a licensed ham radio operator for 76 years. We have a radio station in our basement, with a 50-foot tower in the back field. Tom talked to people all over the world. W1ODC is now a silent key.

I especially enjoyed the stories of his childhood. How his grandmother always made him cube steak sandwiches, when he visited while home from the Navy. He insisted, only he could make them as good as his grandmother, and that was the only thing he ever cooked for me. I loved my life with Tom. He promised me 10 good years, and he gave me 12. Our old age was rewarding, and we thanked God every day for giving us a second chance at love. Rest in Peace Tom De Kay the world is a better place because you were in it.

Thankfulness

There is something to be thankful for

Each and every day

A rippling brook's tranquil sound

In silvery cascades coming down

There is something to be thankful for

Each and every day

When land and sea in harmony

Grace a harvest's crops golden yield

There is something to be thankful for

Each and every day

A walk along this mountain road
Brings flowers for your soul

There is something to be thankful for
Each and every day
I am awestruck by a rainbow's hues
It chases away all the blues

There is something to be thankful for
Each and every day
When strife comes your way
Your fears will never stay

There is something to be thankful for
Each and every day
A light will shine through clouds and rain
To guide you through your pain

There is something to be thankful for
Each and every day
When your heart can sing
Healing will begin

Katharine Bachert Buschbacher De Kay

Photo Reflections

Opa Adam Bachert (2nd from left) WWI
Austrian Army, Italian front, 1918

Elfrieda Kolbe (8) Katharina Bachert (8)
Getting ready for dance performance
at home on Lastina Ulica, Indjija, 1940

Katharina Bachert
First Holy Communion
Indjija, 1938

Unknown, Franz Rilli, Franz & Johann Brucker
Wedding celebration, Indjija, Circa 1936

Franz & Maria Bachert,
Going to church
Alpenstrasse 8A Anif, Austria 1948

Franz & Maria Bachert
Golden wedding celebration
Queens, NY 1977

Best friends (me at left)
Volksdeutches Lager HaimingTirol, 1946

Family getting on train from
Salzburg to Bremerhaven, 1952

Käthe Bachert (16)
Going to church,
Anif, Salzburg, Austria 1948

Katie at the Pepperell switchboard, 1954

Bachert family exploring NYC
1952

The Bachert sisters, Katie & Anne
New York City Christmas 1956

Bernard, Anne De Paul, Katie De Kay,
Adam, Jonathan & Joseph De Paul,
Katie's 80th Birthday celebration
Saluda, NC, 2012

The 3 Bachert Siblings
Anne, Fred & Katie
Caribbean Cruise, Dec 30, 2017

Katie De Kay,
Robert Buschbacher & Debbie
Rowlands Saluda, NC 2010

Robert, Thomas &
Margareth Buschbacher
Cruise, 2012

Jeff, Mathew & Debbie Rowlands,
Matt's graduation
Houston, TX, 2011

Katherine De Kay, Chelsea
(Rowlands) & Ben Sun
Wedding Day, Pecan Springs
Ranch Austin TX 2016

Family Tree

Paternal Grandparents

Grandfather: Adam Bachert

Grandmother: Juliana Flehr Bachert

Maternal Grandparents

Grandfather: Johann Brucker

Grandmother: Katharina Gartner Brucker

Parents

Father: Franz Bachert 1/29/1905 - 6/5/1997

Mother: Maria Brucker Bachert 8/23/1908 – 8/25/2003

Katharina Bachert Buchbacher De Kay 7/11/1932 –

Children

Robert John Buschbacher 10/21/1954 -

Debbie Anne Buschbacher Rowlands 12/22/1960 -

Siblings:

Maria Bachert (2/28/1929 – 12/20/1930)

Franz Bachert (2/27/1931 – 3/26/1931)

Anna Bachert DePaul (7/23/1938 -)

Alfred Franz Bachert (Freddy), (1/28/1948 -)

Husband

Lorenz Buschbacher 9/6/1930 – 5/4/2003

Thomas Joseph De Kay 11/26/1923 – 5/18/2017

Husband Larry's Parents

Father: Lorenz Buschbacher 3/7/1892 – 8/5/1984

Mother: Rosina Rilli Buschbacher 3/19/1902 - 1998

Brother: Valentin Buschbacher 1/22/1923 – 10/29/1980

Made in the USA
Lexington, KY
28 May 2019